THE
MUST HAVE GUIDE
TO GOOGLE ADWORDS

———•◆•———

How to Access Quality Customers
Without Excessive Spending

Table of Contents

Introduction

How this Book will prepare you for War

———◆———

This is your time to shine. Most of you for fair reasons aren't convinced Google Adwords actually works for you and to be quite honest it makes total sense why you feel that way. Very few local based businesses can easily say they've had at least 12 months of straight consistent success with Google Adwords.

1 in 50 can say they've had 12 months of straight success. 1 in 50! How ridiculous is that…!??! This book is here to change this ratio. Now I'm not going to say every single one of the thousands of people who read this will create long term success with Google Adwords because most of you won't apply what I recommend.

You'll either trust your current agency to do it for you and get the same old results you've been getting or you'll actually apply what I recommend. It's the exact same as an attorney advising their client on what to say and what not to say in a deposition. The client will blame the attorney regardless of whether they ignored their attorney's advice or not.

What makes Google Adwords even worse for most businesses especially attorneys is the absurd amount of money you have to spend just for a click. You can easily spend $250 a click as a personal injury attorney. Even worse is the fact I'm about to share a secret which 0.1% of business owners know about Google Adwords.

1% of Digital agencies know about this which makes it even harder for businesses to succeed with Google Adwords when they can't keep up the very high ad spend. The secret is...

Clickfraud Technology

60-70% of your current spend goes on fraudulent/false clicks. Yes, NOT real interested people who want to spend thousands of dollars with you, but false clicks. I knew that would blow your mind. What does that mean? That means let's say you spend $1,000 as a conservative amount on Google Adwords this month. $600-$700 of that isn't even being spent on real people which means you must spend at least $2,000-$4,000 more on average depending on your location just to compete, let alone outrank all of your competitors.

So if you're an attorney or any medical practitioner and you're spending thousands of dollars a month on Google, you're overspending by at least 3-7 times more than you should be for the same results you're acquiring right now. Pretty disturbing right...?

Now that doesn't mean Google Adwords doesn't work because of this. It would be unwise to say that. What I'm saying is you have to overspend by AT LEAST 3-7 times more than you need to in order to hit the amount of patients and cases you're looking to acquire each month.

Of course I'm not starting this book with a problem without a solution and if you're open to it, Clickfraud Technology is what you can use to solve this. Chapter 2 goes much more in depth on this for you which breaks down everything you need to know about clickfraud technology.

It's not something many agencies or business owners know about and it's something Google would like to keep on the down low as much as possible. Also, if you're at a point where you think Google would never do such a thing and there's no way 60-70% of my budget is going on false clicks then stop reading right now and throw the book away. If you're against heavy truth bombs which is the first of many in this book then it's best you stop reading. Yes I'm telling you to literally throw this book away if you can't take the truth.

INSTEAD this book is only for business owners who don't want to waste another second with an agency who can't get them the results they want at the ROI they want. Plain and simple. So if you're one of those business owners then let's keep reading.

One thing I will mention however is outside of clickfraud technology there's 3 main reasons businesses consistently fail with Google Adwords and yes it's the agency's fault you're working with behind this. Also understand, the agency you choose is the one who does the job for you and if you don't choose wisely then all you're going to have for your Google Adwords campaigns is a large dent in your bank account.

3 Main Reasons Most Businesses Fail with Google Adwords

So what are these 3 reasons? The first and arguably most important is the advertising copy a.k.a. ad copy you use. This reason alone is one of the biggest causes of failure throughout Google because you've positioned your business as a commodity from the very start which means you appear to be like every other business.

When I point this out to business owners I speak to, they immediately want to fire their current agency because what's worse as a business owner in having all your value and uniqueness not communicated? You're in business because you can solve a specific problem for people no other competitor can solve as well as you can. So if you don't communicate this throughout your copy it's going to be very difficult for people to know how you can help solve their problem more than a competitor can. Don't worry, we'll be going much deeper into this in a later chapter with picture based examples to show you exactly what I'm talking about.

Understand, if you don't give potential patients and clients a strong specific reason to work with you over a competitor you're going to leave them confused of who to work with. *Confusion kills any good decision being made.* Confusion in many ways is the single greatest reason for poor decisions being made every single day and the second you confuse your potential patients and clients is the second you've lost them.

Let's look at you for one moment. Even looking for a digital agency, every single one of them (almost :D) says they'll help you acquire more patients through Google Adwords, through Facebook etc. But what patients specifically? What age range? How many a month? You can see where I'm going with this and it's not really surprising that you get so frustrated with digital agencies all appearing to be the same.

How the heck are you ever supposed to choose which one to work with when they all seem to do the same thing...?!!? It's the exact same for your potential patients and clients. This is one of the reasons I personally get a lot of enquiries because I specifically say the type of patients I acquire for specific types of businesses and I mention I help businesses *find their specific problem* they solve that they want to communicate to the marketplace. How much easier does that tell you what I do differently and exactly how I can help you? Now I'm not just a digital agency but I'm a digital agency specialising in solving one specific problem, for a specific group of people through a specific medium I.e. Adwords.

The best part is if you see my message and what I do and you don't want help with any of those things then you don't contact me and that works great because we won't be wasting each other's time. This is what you must do with your ad copy. If you don't do this then it's very likely you'll get lots of people calling up trying to ask you for the price when you know they're just going to compare your price to other competitors to see who's the cheapest. That doesn't help anyone.

Ever had a situation where you're trying to explain the value your service can offer a person and all they seem to care about is how cheap you can offer it…? Many of you will quietly be nodding your heads at this. *Fundamentally this is a message problem.* When you communicate the specific problems you solve with your services people often don't question the price because *they know exactly how you can help them.* So, from this point forward only 5-10% of people calling up I.e. time wasters should be asking for the price. Not 50% or even 30% as you must never forget the biggest thing your potential customers care about is solving their specific pain. The bigger the problem the more money a person will pay for a solution.

I've spoken to many businesses who've had tire kickers asking for the price calling up from their Google Adwords 80% of the time. Just imagine how torturous that would be if you spent $5,000 and 80% of the calls from $5000 came from people who had no interest in your value proposition except how cheap you could offer it at…

The truth is, many people are truly interested in your unique solutions and unique value you offer but simply can't tell the difference between you and a competitor. What makes it worse is how simple this is to change as you'll see when we go deeper into this in chapter 16, is the fact many digital agencies don't even ask the business owner how they'd describe their business...

Just imagine randomly deciding to hire a new employee without knowing any of their background, work experience, skills or college degree. How would you know if they'd be a good fit to work at your practice...? You wouldn't know. You'd be hiring based off nothing which is exactly how digital agencies market your business on Adwords. You're lucky to even get the patient or client in the first place from advertising this way.

Now some of you might say "I'm getting patients from this so what's the point in focusing on my specific message". Well, what types of patients or clients do you enjoy working with the most? Most of you will respond with the ones who are truly interested in the unique value you provide to solve a person's specific problem. These patients and cases heavily appreciate the value you provide in the market and will pay significantly more than everyone else and will likely provide handfuls of referrals because you helped them.

Often times I speak with business owners who really don't like their jobs and the minute I acquire them quality patients who resonate with their message they start to find the love they used to have for their profession. Remember, it's difficult to love your profession if you don't have lots of joy in treating the patients and clients you like the most. Let's change that.

Understand, people only really care about what they can get for themselves and if you make it difficult for them to understand exactly what you're going to be solving for them, they'll lose attention. It's not even unfair with humans being this way. If you haven't provided a specific problem you're going to solve then why should the other person work with you? You've made it hard for them to know what you can specifically do for them and as a result you've left them confused.

You can't ever expect to build an empire off Google Adwords when you confuse potential patients & clients. *If anything, you make these people more annoyed and frustrated they can't find a specific solution to what they feel is a specific problem.* You've instead not only framed yourself as a generalist but also framed the potential patient or client as general too. No one wins this way.

The next biggest problem most of you face is quality score. Even without clickfraud technology you can still spend 20-30% less on clicks if you set up your ads to optimise quality score properly. So what is quality score? Well very briefly as there is an entire chapter devoted to this alone, it's simply a specific score Google assigns to your ads to determine how high Google will rank you.

Simply put, your quality score is composed of your Bid on your specific keyword and the relevance of your copy to the keyword. Don't worry if this doesn't make 100% sense. There is an entire chapter on this in chapter 17. So the reason this is a problem is because businesses end up bidding very high amounts of dollars on keywords yet because their relevance of the ad is so low it means they don't rank nearly as highly as they could & spend too much in the process.

For example, if you type in "Chicago Personal Injury Attorney" and then you end up getting "Chicago Divorce Lawyers" showing up then the relevance of that ad is low. When you type anything into Google you as the searcher want exactly what you type in. You don't want anything except what you type in and obviously if you mess this up then Google will punish you severely for this. End result? You won't reach nearly as many quality prospects as you'd like and you'll be severely overspending for those prospects who do enquire with you.

Point is, respect quality score, understand it's value and pay close attention to chapter 17 on quality score so it's really easy for you to implement the advice I give you.

Now at this point, you might possibly be wondering what the third biggest problem is for most businesses using Google Adwords… It's testing. Yes this may seem obvious but it astounds me how few digital agencies actually do this for their clients especially when clients are paying upwards of $5,000 a month.

This is one of the main reasons many business owners don't run ads themselves because of the relentless nature you must have to keep testing new ideas all the time because if you don't then your ads eventually stop converting. Your ads either don't work right away from the beginning or they start working well and then stop working. This is because testing stopped or there wasn't any testing whatsoever.

Understand, you cannot succeed at Adwords long term with your business if you don't test enough. Eventually your ads just stop working and if you don't change them then you end up spending money for the sake of it without any real return on your investment.

Now as I'm sure you know there's an entire chapter devoted to testing alone so for now understand this: success with Google Adwords is completely proportionate to the amount of times you've tested. Seriously. A person who tests 50 different ads has a much higher chance of success than someone who tests 3 ads. I'm not saying every single business has to test 50 ads right away but what I'm saying is be willing to test more than you originally anticipated.

You cannot expect to just test based off what you assume will work. You can only test based off what the data gives you and more times than not you'll find what you thought would work often times doesn't work. Instead you saved yourself thousands of dollars by staying objective rather than just assuming it would work. So with Adwords, don't assume. If you learn anything from this book let it be this, never ever assume you know what will work and what won't. Google can be very surprising and if you're not prepared you'll lose money faster than you can say Google.

It's critical before you work with any agency you've completely understood all 3 concepts I've briefly spoken about above. Not having one of them done properly can lose you thousands of dollars in money and your time working with the wrong agency. The best example when I explain this is what happens if you've been in a car accident and you're looking for a chiropractor to treat you.

You'll often times pick a chiropractor who's a family friend or go off a referral and trust their judgement without fundamentally looking into what types of treatment you need for your specific accident. Not understanding this can result in serious pain and trauma.

Now that doesn't mean you go out there and have to learn everything I've said about Google Adwords as fitting everything into this book would far exceed 1000 pages. But what I'm saying is understand these 3 important concepts because once you do and you get the agency you're considering working with to talk about them then you'll see 95% of these "expert" agencies will fall beneath your current knowledge base.

Even if you read 25% of this book you'll know more than 95% of ad agencies running Google Adwords. Seriously. I know it's a bit of a shock to hear that because you expect these agencies to be true experts in what they do when they charge $2,000 minimum a month of your money. The fact is 95% of them have no real idea of how to run successful long term campaigns and the faster you grasp this the faster you'll be able to hire a marketing agency who you feel truly knows what they're doing.

Just one more thing on this, many business owners like to seek references from agencies because they like to see the agency has had success in the past. But they fail to grasp the fact each business is different and requires a slightly different solution each time depending on their situation. Remember, Google Adwords must never be cookie cutter and just because an Agency had success with one business doesn't mean they'll have success with you.

Often times testimonials are completely misrepresented to showcase results when in reality the business in the testimonial had a completely different situation to yours. For example the business owner as a reference may've been spending $10,000 a month in ad spend, may've been in an less competitive city than you. Either way the point is each reference and testimonial is different so success with one business owner doesn't mean success with another. The only way to ensure your business is successful long term with Google Adwords is by having a completely customised solution with an agency who is prepared to relentlessly test for you.

If they only test a few things every month then forget it. Even if you get some results to start with then there's no guarantee you'll keep getting results long term. Anyway, let's move on right now.

Now in this introduction having pushed your mind ready to use Google Adwords very profitably for your business, let's jump right into the first chapter. If you're not ready to have your hat blown off to all the secrets I'm going to share then take a break and come back later. I guarantee in the introduction alone there's at least one fact I've mentioned you've never heard anywhere else before.

Get ready, let's dive into this right now.

Callum Davies

Orlando, Florida, November 2018

Chapter 1

Designing Your Mind
to Tune into the Psychology of
Search

———◆———

As we all know every single online advertising platform has a slightly different psychological buying process. For example, Facebook advertising is all about pattern interruption because people are on Facebook to be social and get away from their lives. They don't want to be hard sold on anything even if it's something they've been looking to buy. They don't want that kind of disturbance. However, trying to get people to call from your Facebook ads isn't the best strategy. Lead forms are far superior.

How Your Potential Customers are Searching for Your Business

Now, moving over to Google Adwords you must remember people are searching for a specific solution to their problem. You don't need to necessarily pattern interrupt people because the searcher is looking for a solution. This is one of the reasons when done right Google Adwords for any local business can be the most effective paid traffic source they use. Therefore it's of paramount importance you pay attention to what I'm about to say.

Google Adwords is all about having the best offer to suit the searcher's needs. The better the offer the higher chance you have of the searcher giving you a call and doing business with you. Sounds simple right? Well it's much easier than you think yet for whatever reasons very few businesses differentiate themselves properly based on their offer. This is something we'll go in much more depth later in the copy section later in chapter 16 as this one principle can quite literally make or break your entire presence on Adwords altogether.

Why Your Potential Customers are Searching for Your Business

Let's talk a bit more about why people search in the first place. Interesting question right? Well some of you may think that people are searching for information and are searching for new products and services to buy. Well, the fact is most people either consciously or unconsciously are searching because they have a specific problem they want the answer to. Imagine the last time you searched for something on Google. You weren't just searching for information, you were searching for information to help you solve the problem you were struggling with. Once you had the right solution, you stopped searching because you had the answer you needed.

It's the exact same for any searcher looking for a solution your business can provide. However, it's critical right now you start to get really specific about what problems you actually solve because if you don't know then you can't expect the searcher to work that out for you. Thinking takes a LOT of energy and the last thing a person will do is figure out exactly how you can help them. NO, you must figure this out and do it right now. Once you've done that, decide on ONE solution for each service you feel is the best for people needing your help.

Once you've done that Adwords becomes much easier to have success with because you're different from the very beginning. You're not just offering a free or paid consultation but instead offering something so much more. The searcher knows right away if they're the type of patient or client who would be a good fit for you.

The Importance Aligning Your Goals, The Searcher's Goals & Google's Goals

So, let's now dive into aligning your Goals with the searchers goals and most importantly with Google's goals. Understand, there is a 3 way street here with you, your searcher and Google themselves. Many people start to do well in terms of creating a great offer for potential patients but fail in understanding Google's goals and so massively under perform.

It all stems from understanding Google is a business just like yours. They make 90% of their revenue from their advertising and if any person isn't playing by the rules then of course they're going to dismiss their ads completely. No one wants this considering how many potential patients are searching on Google every month. So, Google themselves like Ads that are getting the highest click through rate meaning the amount of people clicking on your ads because they simply make more money. If your ads don't get clicked on then Google don't have a good reason to promote your ads to more people. (Yes they actually do this).

As I've said before, your click through rate will come down to your ad copy which is a whole separate topic we go through in chapter 16 we'll get into later and for now understand ad copy's importance. If

14

your ad copy isn't very good then your ads will severely suffer. Plain and simple. There's no way around it.

You'll end up paying far more money than you have to which will limit your ROI in the process and if anything limit your effectiveness on Google as a whole. The biggest mistake I see now is large local businesses who think they can get away from simply outspending all their competitors. Now while this may work against most people, it still leaves them very vulnerable to you beating them because they're not aligning themselves with what Google wants and that is an ad which not only gets a lot of clicks but also one which is highly relevant to the keyword. More on this later.

If you're going into Google thinking you can just outspend your competitors then you're going to be in for a crazy ride because eventually you will lose. All it takes is one competitor to understand Google Adwords properly and sooner or later they'll outrank you whilst spending 3-7 times less than you're spending. Now I'm not saying Google don't want you to spend lots of money because of course they do. But what they care about more is an ad getting clicked on a lot because they understand this will lead to much higher profitability in the long run.

They know those businesses are going to be able to advertise for much longer and of course if a business is getting at least a 10-1 return from Google then everyone wins.

So start by understanding Google's goal of an ad with a higher click through rate and then start figuring out what your potential patient's goal would be when they search. Do they want more information relating to a problem they have? Do they want a service which can solve a specific problem they have? Do they just want a product they can take home with them to help solve a specific problem? Once you've established this then you can fit your goals right in between. You've started thinking about the 2 other parties before you've even thought about yourself and in many ways that is the start of very high quality marketing.

High quality marketing is always customer focused. Not focused on how good you are as a company or how good your product or service is. Never ever forget this and you'll be better than 95% of all your competitors.

Ads aren't Ads When You're Providing Information

Now as we close the end of this chapter it's critical we briefly touch on the importance of how you've framed your ad. What is framing? Framing is simply the meaning of what you're describing e.g. You could frame your service as saving a person money or you could frame your service as saving a person from bankruptcy. The service is still fundamentally the same at the end of the day but it differs depending on how you frame it as a frame gives a specific meaning. A meaning then determines how a person will perceive your advertising.

Now, one of the biggest mistakes and biggest hatreds of the human population is reading ads. They know right away whenever a business advertises they're going to get sold on something and people hate to get sold on anything. BUT remember the good news is people love to buy & humans also love help with specific problems they're experiencing. They want to feel complete independence they made the decision to buy something themselves rather than feeling they were sold. So if humans hate ads then how are you supposed to advertise on Google if all you see are ads...?!?!

Really great question. Understand the good news is people don't hate ads when they're being given helpful information. When a person is given helpful information that's highly relevant to solving their problem they'll read your ad from start to finish. At the end of the day your potential patients and clients just want the solution to their specific problem and if you're framing your ad to be offering information rather than selling them on a service then you're winning already.

So one of the many things businesses on Google Adwords offer is some kind of consultation. A consultation is great because you're giving away good information to the person so they then can optimally decide if they want to work with you for the full service you're offering. However, most businesses don't frame a consultation this way.

Instead when people see "free consultation" or even a consultation they immediately think they're going to get sold. If you don't take control and start influencing people's perceptions from the beginning then they're going to be left to their own perception which in many cases isn't going to benefit you or your business.

This is why it's absolutely critical on Adwords and your landing pages you reinforce exactly what they'll get for free in the consultation itself even if they have to pay for the consultation. You frame the consultation as important information each person will receive to determine if it makes sense to work together on the full service. If it doesn't make sense then the person will still get a free consultation out of it. *Remember, people don't mind in spending money on quality solutions.* What they fear and don't like is the feeling they're going to be sold when they go in for their consultation because in their mind they feel they've lost control. Understand, people HATE to lose control.

Therefore you frame the consultation as you helping them figure out if your service can work for them. That way the prospect thinks "Well either way I'm getting a lot of quality information out of it" and in turn you're creating a no lose situation for the prospect. Once you've done this, most potential patients won't feel as though there's a downside to giving you a call. Plus most businesses when you come in for a consultation will ask the person simple questions anyway to determine the person's current position.

They won't really sell them and INSTEAD the person from answering their questions will sell themselves which is key.

So, start framing your entire campaigns and advertising around this principle. Start to apply this right away before you've launched any campaigns. I'm telling you, if you get this wrong or skip this step completely you're putting yourself in a situation of being vulnerable to competitors easily taking business away from you. If they win business from you through great strategy then fair enough. But if they win business because you made it too easy then that's just humiliating.

Let's now jump into the next chapter on Clickfraud technology and knowing exactly why so few elite advertisers even know about it's existence and how it can turn a campaign achieving nothing to one achieving a 10-1 return extremely quickly!

Chapter 2

How Clickfraud technology Will Prevent You From Drowning

———◆———

This chapter will completely blow your mind of why you're currently getting royally screwed over by Google and EXACTLY what will happen to your campaigns if you don't implement this technology. So to understand this, let's talk about how your current Google data isn't accurate. Yes you heard me correctly, IT'S NOT ACCURATE.

Why You NEED Clickfraud Technology

Whenever you advertise on Google you're looking for clicks because clicks lead the prospect to a landing page which eventually can lead to a sale. That's all well and good. Everyone understands that. What you may not know however is right now if you're advertising on Google then you're overspending by at least 3 times more than you need to be for the current results you're getting. For example, you may be spending $2,000 to hit 10 patients a month when in reality you could be spending $600-$800 to acquire those same 10 patients.

How is that even possible? Well I can tell you it's not really down to your competitors driving your budget up. That's about 5-10% of the equation here.

The real reason behind this is Google themselves. Right now as we speak, 60-70% of all your clicks aren't even real people clicking. They're bots and hackers roaming around on Google clicking on anything and everything to drive your budget up because remember, Google makes more money when you're getting more clicks. The more clicks you're getting which you perceive to be good the higher chance you'll keep advertising on Google.

You think well If "I'm getting more clicks then my ads must be working" and therefore if they appear to be working then it only makes sense to keep advertising on Google a little while longer as long as it keeps "working" well.

It's actually *terrifying* how few advertising agencies know about this. Seriously, if you're getting a 3-1 return right now you could easily get a 9-1 return just by implementing the clickfraud technology. It's because you aren't aware of what you're missing out on that you don't feel a huge need to at least triple your results. Now you know. Here's a challenge for you.

When you explain this to your current advertising agency 99% of them will tell you this isn't true and Google are such a great company and would never do this to their customers. Those are the agencies you fire because they don't care about the truth and the truth in this case could prevent you from losing at least 3 times more than you need to on Google Adwords every single month.

Now pay close attention to the images below. What you can see here is a picture of a client's Google Analytics data I pulled from a month without clickfraud technology before I started working with them &

a client I just started working with implementing Clickfraud right away just to prove my point. How can you possibly explain having 31 clicks and only 20 users…? You really think 10 + users clicked on the ad more than once… When I showed this to the client they were mind blown. They thought Google was a super honest company too. What you see below is in many ways one of the biggest reasons you must be using clickfraud technology in your Adwords campaigns. It's because the data is completely false which means if you think an ad is doing well and getting lots of clicks the natural thing to do is double down on the ad to get even more results.

Campaign / Campaign ID	Acquisition				Behaviour		
	Clicks	Cost	CPC	Users	Sessions	Bounce Rate	Pages/Session
	31 [illegible]	US$160.82 [illegible]	US$5.19 [illegible]	20 [illegible]	24 [illegible]	100.00% [illegible]	1.00 [illegible]
1. Bellvue Campaign [illegible]	31 [illegible]	US$160.82 [illegible]	US$5.19	20 [illegible]	24 [illegible]	100.00%	1.00

Figure 2.1. showing 11 more clicks over users demonstrating clickfraud.

Campaign / Campaign ID	Acquisition				Behaviour		
	Clicks	Cost	CPC	Users	Sessions	Bounce Rate	Pages/Session
	46 [illegible]	US$144.88 [illegible]	US$3.15 [illegible]	40 [illegible]	47 [illegible]	87.23% [illegible]	1.04 [illegible]
1. Charlotte Chiropractor [illegible]	46 [illegible]	US$144.88 [illegible]	US$3.15	38 [illegible]	45 [illegible]	91.11%	1.09

Figure 2.2. Showing 46 clicks for 40 users showing the impact of clickfraud technology by making sure each click is an actual person.

BUT, as the data in almost every case is completely wrong you'd be doubling down on an ad which wasn't nearly as effective as you thought it was. What does this even mean?

It means you'd overspend on an ad which would drain your budget even more. Remember, we're not advertising just to get new quality patients and clients. We're advertising because we want to spend as little as possible to ensure we secure the greatest return possible. What's startling is how few businesses use Google Adwords this way. They think they can just throw a bunch of money at Google and expect Google to reward them handsomely. Here's a fact, IT DOESN'T WORK THAT WAY.

What Happens if you don't use Clickfraud Technology?

So what's going to happen if you decide to ignore my advice and not implement clickfraud technology? 1. You're guaranteed to be losing AT LEAST 3 times more money on Adwords than necessary to achieve the specific result you want each month. That is a fact.

I'm not telling you to implement clickfraud technology if you don't want to but what I am saying is prepare to face the consequences if you don't implement clickfraud technology. To make matters worse your data from Google is going to be completely ruined because you're getting clicks which aren't even real people so you'll end up spending money in the wrong places. This means you're not spending money on the ads your potential patients will respond to which means they'll just go to a competitor of yours instead. Once again you've made it too easy for a competitor to take business off you.

Remember, you're not on Google to spend money on the wrong people and worthless clicks. You're advertising to find the right people who work well with your business and this certainly won't happen very well if you don't know which ads to double down on. So you have these enormous leverage points where you can spend 5% of the money you're spending on Google right now and get 95% of the results. But you won't achieve this if you don't have *accurate data* to work with.

So some of you who like to move fast in business are looking for what brand of clickfraud technology would be good to implement. Click Cease is personally a good recommendation to start with and was the very first piece of technology I used when I first started with it. You can even get a free trial as shown in Figure 2.1 so I'd strongly recommend starting there. The support of Click Cease is fairly good as well so if you have any obstacles you're trying to overcome then they'll help you very easily. Now this isn't the technology I use any more and if you don't mind working with me then I'll show you which technology I use now. Either way start with Click Cease, get in quality data right away and look at the comparison yourself. It's going to blow your mind to pieces!

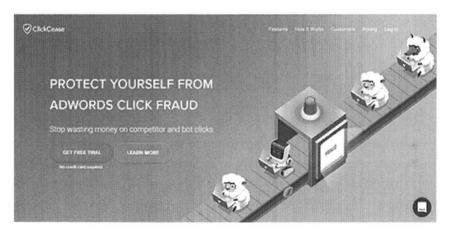

Figure 2.3. Showing ClickCease clickfraud technology.

Why Very Few Advertising Agencies Know the World Class Secrets About Clickfraud

Now, it's likely many of you are thinking how the heck I know about this and why your current agency hasn't told you about this. The reason comes down to research. This information is out there for the whole world to see. For instance Google a few years ago was fined 90 million dollars for clickfraud. That information is in the open space for anyone and everyone to go out there and look at. Yet most people don't because they work off the assumption Google is a great company and wouldn't do anything like I've proven to you in this chapter.

On top of which Clickfraud technology isn't the cheapest thing in the world for most agencies and they'd rather take the risk of not knowing about this than spending more money to help their clients. Now as I said before, I'm not saying if you don't use clickfraud technology you won't get any results whatsoever on Google. That's not what I'm saying at all. I'm saying your effectiveness on Google will be severely limited without clickfraud technology. If you're going to do any kind of advertising the last thing you want to be is limited. *Average businesses stay in the limited zone.* Brilliant businesses move into the expansive zone which is what clickfraud technology allows you to do.

So there you have it. This information on Clickfraud technology has remained a secret among my personal clients for a long period of time and every single one was shocked at how surprising this is to hear. Now, the information is right in front of you so you can right away implement this kind of technology into your campaigns. This works with both the Google display network and works very well with Bing ads too as both platforms here are extremely important in scaling out the advertising of any business.

We'll go into Bing in much more depth later but just so you know you'll want to apply clickfraud technology to your campaigns on other search advertising networks too. The only platform clickfraud technology doesn't really work with is Facebook which has their own strategic ways of making money off you that you're likely not aware of. Maybe I'll talk about that in the next book I write for you.

Get ready for the next phase of mastering Adwords where we'll discuss why you must only give friends account access to your Adwords account and exactly how to ensure *you keep maximum control* of the account whenever you hire a new digital agency.

Chapter 3

Only Allow Friends
Account Access

———◆———

Now this chapter is very important. It's not the most glamorous but the good news is it's absolutely critical to you running successful Adwords campaigns. This is also the area where the vast majority of business owners fail to learn because for whatever reason they take an agency's advice without doing their own research. That's the same as me going to a dentist, believing that I need veneers and just taking their word for it. Whether I needed veneers isn't important. What's important is the fact I didn't do my own research to see how accurate the advice was I received. So let's dive right into this.

How to Succeed Creating an Adwords Account

First off, you must not only know how to create an Adwords account but actually create one. Most businesses work with an agency's ad account and don't advertise off the business owner's account. What this means is when the business wants to stop working with the agency it can't because it means the business won't have a quality account to run ads off. As a result you've completely lost control so it means you're limited on what your options are which isn't a good situation for you. So, what's the solution to this? Simply, create your own ad account which I'll take you through below in the different images presented. This way you'll know exactly how to make an ad account instead of trying to figure it out for yourself.

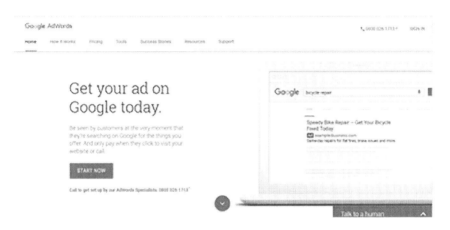

Figure 3.1 showing you the homepage of Google Adwords.

You must first go to www.adwords.google.com and you'll see the exact same page as you see in figure 3.1. Once you're at this page and I'd strongly recommend Google chrome or Firefox over all other browsers, 2. Click the green "Start Now" button where you'll get taken to the same page as figure 3.2 right below.

Figure 3.2 Showing you how to set up your Google Adwords account.

This is very simple also. Simply put your best email address for your Adwords account in and make sure to type in your website. But remember, it's much better when you set up your account if you use a Gmail account as it's much easier to access because if you for whatever reason lose your email, it's much easier to get it back with Gmail. You don't have to follow my advice but be warned. Couldn't be simpler so far could it?

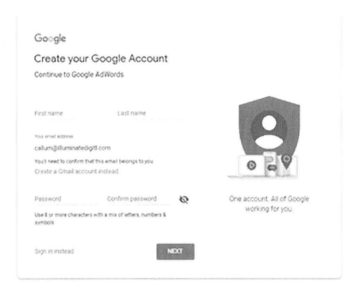

Figure 3.3 showing you the final page before full Google Adwords account access.

Figure 3.3 is the final page you'll fill out before you're given full access to your Adwords account. Simply fill out your first name, last name, email and then create a password. I would recommend you as the owner of the business setting this up in your name rather than an office manager doing so. Office manager's can easily leave anytime and leave you in a very annoying situation so take that into consideration. Once you've done this you've created your ad account and you're ready to start inviting people to work on your account on your behalf if necessary.

Figure 3.4 Showing you distributing Account Access.

Giving Account Access to Others Without Losing Control

Now, let's talk about sharing and giving access to your account if you decide it's best for your business if you let someone else run your Google Adwords for you. Now you're already ahead of 90% of business owners who don't have their own account after creating yours. Now a word of warning, many agencies will want to work off their account and will demand you agree with them. While it may be better to do this in the short term because they've already spent thousands of dollars on their account already, I strongly recommend not doing it.

You're building their ad account which is good for them but you're not building your own. So always insist the agency run ads out of your ad account. Sometimes with clients they want very results in the first 48 hours and that's fine so you could always run ads out of their account and yours at the same time. That way you're heavily benefiting.

So as you can see in figure 3.4, 5. you want to click the tire icon in the top right hand side of your ad account which will drop down a list

29

of options. 6. You then want to click "Account settings" and then you'll want to 7. Click "Account Access" on the left hand side of your screen. Once you've done that you'll be on the exact same page as figure 3.4.

Don't worry you're almost done. 8. You must click the big red button on the same page and you'll then be able to add a person via their email and name to your ad account as shown in figure 3.5 right below. I would recommend you setting the person you're adding to the account as admin if they're running campaigns for you.

This way you still have complete control of your account so you can check what campaigns are being run, what ad copy is being used, if the ad copy is in line with the message of your business etc.

Once you've sent them an invitation, 9. they'll get an email in their inbox saying you've invited them and finally 10. they'll accept the invitation which you can finalise on the same page as figure 3.4 just above. Now you've successfully made your own ad account, added the agency to your ad account and still retain complete control. How is it beneficial to you if you can't always see what ads are being run on your behalf? Well it isn't.

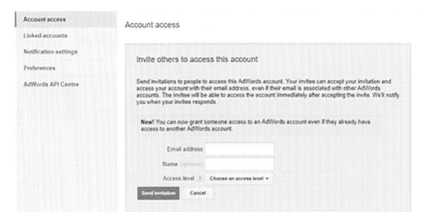

Figure 3.5 showing you how to Invite others to access your account.

Now, you must not only understand how to set up payments but also understand how Google bills you. The last thing you want is a massive bill from Google not having realised how they've charged you. Trust me, this happens to at least 5 out of 10 business owners because they aren't aware of the information I'm about to share with you right here.

Figure 3.6 showing you how to access your billing settings.

Setting Up Adwords Billing & Payments

As you can see in figure 3.6, this is exactly how to reach your billing settings. You must 1. Click into your ad account itself otherwise the billing and payments tab in figure 3.6 won't be given to you as an option. Once there, 2. You want to click "Billing & payments" and then you'll be taken to put in your card information and all other details which are important.

Word of warning though, I would strongly recommend you using either your Amex card or any other credit card you may have. It's far more effective being billed this way than using any kind of debit card which now brings me to the final stage of this chapter: How Google bills you.

You Must Understand How Google Bills You

Personally one of the easiest ways to be billed which YOU CONTROL is paying Google through a threshold. This means you get billed when you hit a specific amount so you don't go over I.e. you can set a limit of $350 which means you'll only be charged that. You won't get charged anymore until you turn on your ads again. This way it's easier for you to not spend thousands of dollars in a month if your ads aren't working.

Now, if you're a person who'd prefer to try a different angle, Google will just bill you after every 30 days. This isn't a bad method to pay Google but it does mean you have to monitor your spending much more if you're wanting to reach at least a 10-1 return. Unless you can truly trust the agency you're using to control your budget properly then stick with a billing threshold. Trust me, you'll thank me later.

So we've reached the end of this chapter and I truly hope you got value from it. Let's move onto the inner game mindset behind Adwords so you'll be able to set crucial goals you can work with and actually achieve. When you have goals it becomes much easier to know if you're hitting your targets, or you're failing completely. Let's explore this together now.

Chapter 4

Adwords Goals Push You Towards Market Domination

———————◆———————

This perhaps is one of the most important chapters in this entire book. Seriously don't take what I'm about to say light heartedly.

Following this advice will make a serious difference to your Adwords campaigns and the concept itself can dramatically improve your own life for the better. The answer…? The best in the industry set goals. This topic was inspired by Brad Geddes in his incredible book "Advanced Google Adwords" which I'd strongly recommend you read if you want to learn every tiny detail of Adwords itself. Either way, it's a fantastic book and worth every single penny.

The Reason Your Entire Campaign Rests on the Goals You Set

So what are Adwords goals? Simply put, goals in Adwords are you targets you're looking to hit in order to achieve the specific ROI you're wanting for the month. An example of a goal could be e.g. Cost Per Conversion must be $3 for every conversion. If you're hitting this or below then that's fantastic. If you're paying more per conversion than this then you know you need serious improvement.

Knowing this piece of information alone can seriously help your ability to run focused Adwords. Otherwise what happens is you run a bunch of campaigns and you have to guess whether they've achieving the type of success you're looking for. That's not a pretty situation for any business owner is it?

How to Set Remarkable Goals for Google Adwords

It's important you set goals in the most critical aspects of your Google campaigns such as 1. Cost Per Conversion/Phone Call, 2. Click Through Rate & 3. Budget required to reach the specific end goal you're looking for. Once you've set these 3 goals it becomes much easier to you what a successful campaign looks like from the inside. Not just the outside.

If you decide you want 5 patients or clients this month from your campaigns then great. But you haven't specified what metrics you're looking to hit in order to reach those 5 patients. Make sense so far?

Any campaign can hit 5 patients a month but it's pointless if you don't know if you'd like to pay $500 for those patients or $100 for those patients. As a result you won't know what constitutes real success and real failure in Google. Any agency could get you 5 patients and so could another. But if you don't have a target budget of what to spend and not a rough number, then it'll be harder for you to know which agency did better.

We're not in the game to guess who's better. We're in the game to know for sure who's 100% better. When you know this you'll be able to pick which agency is going to be the best for your business and as a result acquire far more patients at a much cheaper cost.

Now, some of you might start to ask how the heck do you even set metric based goals in the first place? That's a great question and a super easy one to answer. You must first know what you'd like to spend a month to acquire a specific number of patients. Once you've done know this you can check the actual cost per click prices on any tool such as SEM Rush or SpyFu or even the Google Keyword Planner and compare from there.

Once you've done that, you can figure out how many clicks it's going to take for a phone call and then how many phone calls to book an appointment etc. Often times for many of you, you won't know this if you've not advertised on Google before. Many of you won't be experienced with this if you haven't worked with an agency who's been tracking this for you.

This way you can determine exactly how much I'm required to spend to reach a specific amount of patients at the maximum cost you want to pay. From there you can set more ambitious goals to spend 3-5 times less than the actual maximum you'd need to spend to exceed those goals.

It can get really fun trying to beat your own goals every single month. Remember, don't skip this part. Of course it's easy to learn about Adwords, Quality Score, Clickfraud technology and copy and want to get started right away. But that wouldn't be wise at all.

To run successful campaigns every month you must first know what a successful campaign even looks like to you. If you don't know what a successful campaign looks like then you could run Adwords campaigns for a year and have no idea how successful it is or how successful it could be.

All you'd know is the amount of patients it's bringing you which isn't good enough if you're wanting to beat your top competitors. So please, don't take this information lightly and make sure before you run any campaigns you get very clear with your 3 metric based goals. Once you've done that you can start beating those goals every single month and most importantly have a lot more fun doing so.

Just so you know, the next chapter about the Google Sandbox will completely blow your mind. I'm fairly sure less than 3 authors on Google have spoken openly about the Google sandbox. It's not surprising considering the top Adwords experts are endorsed by Google so they couldn't talk about this stuff even if they wanted to. Let's dive face first into this.

Chapter 5

You Don't Want to Play in the Google Sandbox

———◆———

This is in many ways besides Clickfraud technology is the least known topic in Google Adwords itself. It's truly scary how few people not only know about this but communicate it to business owners so they know what's going on. So pay close attention to everything I'm going to say in this entire chapter because if there's one thing which will break your campaigns in half the fastest, it's the Google Sandbox. Now I'm sure none of us are thinking a real in person sandbox but the picture below in figure 5.1 portrays what you're going to be facing when first advertising on Google.

Figure 5.1 showing a sandbox.

What is the Google Sandbox?

Simply put, it's an imaginary box Google first puts every single new account into severely limiting the amount of people you can reach by as much as 75%. This means before you've launched any Ads you're only going to be able to reach 25% of the potential audience you're going after. Doesn't sound pretty does it? Of course it doesn't.

You're essentially trapped in this imaginary box for what could be up to 6 months unless you know how to get out of it as quickly as possible.

Once again, many of you might be thinking well what's the reason Google even have a sandbox in the first place? Well as I've said before, Google is a business just like yours. They have rules & policies and don't want to appear bad in front of their customers if an unethical advertiser starts ripping people off.

So, Google created the sandbox to:
1. Make even more money out of you.

2. Use this period to ensure you're an ethical advertiser who wants to help their new customers.

Google at the end of the day can't take the risk of an unethical advertiser heavily running ads and ripping people off because this would make Google look bad. Then news gets around and Google lose a severe amount of revenue because people start to move more towards Facebook, Bing and other smaller platforms.

Now as I said above, Google wants to maximise the amount of money they make out of you which is similar to you upselling your current patients and clients. Now they may not do it in the most ethical way but they still do it and most importantly you know what's coming when you first start to advertise on Google. As a result, the sandbox prevents many business owners from starting their own account because agencies use this piece of information to scare business owners into working on the agency's account.

Now, this is great in the short term but in the long term it's far more beneficial for you to have your own account because you own it and have full control over it. Every dollar you then spend on the account which improves the effectiveness of your business in Google's eyes. They start to view your business as proven and ethical and as a result will start to show your ads to a much wider reach of your audience which is what we're after. We don't want to be stuck fighting over only 25% of our audience.

What Happens if We Don't Break Out of the Google Sandbox?

Well, you don't make a great ROI for one and it's likely you'll start to believe advertising on Google is a complete waste of time. This in turn means you'll stop using one of the top 2 most important online marketing methods for growing your business. (SEO is the other). We don't want that. You'll look just like the person below in figure 5.2. Banging your head against the wall over and over again with nothing to show for it except frustration and a smaller bank account. It's not an ideal situation for any business.

Figure 5.2 showing a man banging his head against the wall.

But, it's very important despite the sandbox placed on every new account you still advertise off your new account. It's not very beneficial for you if you never start to advertise off your own account in the long run. You don't want to lose control over whether you can leave working with an agency or not because your Adwords won't be running off their highly functioning account anymore. Take control back which you'll be able to do when you learn exactly how to break out of the sandbox which we'll discuss right here.

So it's not as difficult as you might think to break out of the sandbox. However, it will be a tedious & repetitive process so you're ready to deal with what's in front of you.

Step by Step How to Break Out of the Google Sandbox

First off, it's likely if you've never advertised before you're not going to get much out of it in the first 30-45 days on a budget below $3,000. You may get a few calls here and there and it might lead to some more patients for you but at the end of the day it's not going to generate 10+ new quality patients for you on a lower budget in the first 30-45 days. Now what I will say is breaking out of the sandbox with most agencies takes at least 90 days so fortunately for you I've managed to get this process down to 30-60 days instead. I know you'll thank me later for this.

On top of which, even with clickfraud technology which by the way is something you don't want to use when breaking out of the sandbox. Yes that sounds super hypocritical considering I've been talking about how important it is but the clickfraud technology will lower your Click through rate. Normally that's good because you know all your clicks are coming from real people, not bots or hackers. But the biggest factor in getting out of the sandbox as quickly as possible is by having the highest click through rate as possible. The higher your click through rate the higher your quality score and the higher your quality score the more value Google will see in your Ads so naturally they'll want to show your ads to more people.

Remember, we want Google working with us rather than against us. The more Google is working against us the longer this process is going to take.

So, how do we raise our click through rate as quickly as possible without breaking Google's terms of service? The first thing comes down to how often our Ads are showing and how many people have the potential to see our ads. You'll see below in figure 5.3 how you're able to adjust the radius of your ads which you'll want to do to at least 30 miles.

Yes that may be too far for many businesses but it's more important you get out of the sandbox as quickly as possible. Sometimes Google like your ads so much you only have to spend $200 to get out of the sandbox. However, it's important you give your ads the greatest chance of reaching the highest amount of people possible. If you have above $3,000 to break out of the sandbox within the first 30 days then target the entire city which is also shown below in figure 5.3 so you have that option there as well.

Figure 5.3 showing Google radius targeting.

Now, of course that's not the only way to raise your click through rate. You want to ensure the schedule of your ads is set to 24 hours demonstrated below in figure 5.4. As you can see, normally you'd set the schedule of your ads to shown only in normal office hours.

However this time you want your ads to show to as many people as possible as often as possible. This is going to dramatically increase your chances of breaking out of the sandbox as quickly as possible. Now at this point, some of you may be thinking how would I know if I broke out of the sandbox? Well it's a good question because Google don't send you a notification when you've broken out of it. That would be wonderful if they did, but sadly they don't. As a result, you must pay attention to the "Impressions" you're getting inside of your account. You can see the impressions tab below in figure 5.5.

Figure 5.4 showing you how to schedule your ads.

Figure 5.5 showing you the impressions tab inside your Google Adwords account.

So what are impressions? Impressions are simply when an ad is displayed in front of a person on their phone, tablet, computer etc. For every impression you know how many people have viewed your ad and as a result your click through rate is divided by the amount of people who click your ad with the amount of people who've seen your ad. Very simple really.

The point is, when your impressions in your account start to go through the roof you'll know you've broken out of the sandbox. Of course your clicks will naturally start to go up but what's most important is to pay attention to the amount of impressions you've started getting. When you know this information you'll start to climb out of the sandbox much faster. Of course this sounds like a lot of work and one could argue it is but the good news is it's much better to go through this process as quickly as possible than not having your own Adwords account at all. What's arguably worse is the business owners who do have their own account, break out of the sandbox by spending thousands of dollars and then stop using their account because the agency they work with persuaded the business owner to use the agency's account instead.

This is perhaps one of the worst situations when working with another agency because you've already spent thousands of dollars with Google and when you stop using your account Google will put you right back into another sandbox again. Of course the sandbox won't be as severe and annoying as the first one but you'll still have to spend money again without getting anything for it.

So remember, when you advertise on your Google account, NEVER STOP USING IT. Even if your budget is very limited for external reasons then just spend $100 a month to keep the account alive. If you don't keep the account alive and let your account die you only have yourself to blame when you pump money into it again and you see nothing for it. It's like putting money into a vending machine over and over again without getting anything for it. It wastes your money and most importantly wastes your time.

To conclude this chapter it might be helpful to review what you've just read once more to ensure you're very comfortable in getting out of the sandbox. A very small percentage of you may not believe the sandbox even exists and if that's the case then I urge you to put down this book right now. All I can say is up to this point, you as the reader know more about how to master Google Adwords than 95% of agencies and business owners put together.

It's a shocking statistic when you think about how many marketers proclaim themselves as "experts" at their job. Now you know better.

Let's now dive into tracking codes because one thing I can tell you is if you set your 3 metric based goals but don't track your Adwords campaigns then you definitely won't be able to tell if your campaigns are successful or not. You'll be the blind leading the blind. See you on the other side.

Chapter 6

Tracking Codes Keep Your Campaigns Alive

———————◆———————

This is once again going to be an extremely important chapter for you to pay attention to because if you don't track your results then it's going to be very difficult for you to know whether your campaigns are working or not. It's one thing to know what your 3 metric based goals are but if you have no way of tracking them then you're going to struggle in determining how successful your campaigns are.

Almost everyone gets this wrong because people don't pay attention and think they know everything so it's critical you pay attention to everything I say here in this chapter.

What are Tracking Codes?

So to start with, what are tracking codes…? Tracking codes are simply specific pieces of code in every Google account which allow you to retarget your ads back to certain parts of your audience and allow you to track how many converted actions you've received. Just so you know, you don't need to know code or anything like that to use these codes properly. You only need to know where to place these codes and ensure they're installed properly to get the maximum benefit. Once you've established this then you're set to go. So let's start with the remarketing code.

I'm not going to go super in depth on remarketing here because there's a whole separate chapter on remarketing but all you need to know now is why remarketing is important and where to place the code.

The Different Types of Tracking Codes which are Essential to Your Adwords Success

Remarketing allows you to show your ad over and over again to specific visitors who've visited your site or landing page and haven't taken any action. For example a visitor goes to your landing page but then gets distracted and doesn't give you a call. Normally for most landing pages it takes 5-12 attempts for a person to finally call and in our case with optimised copy and landing page structure the average will be between 1-5 attempts. So if that's the average amount of touches you need it's quite literally campaign suicide to not show your ads in front of these people again. These visitors never once said they didn't like your ad. They simply left the page either due to boredom which I'll talk about in chapter 16 or they simply got distracted which happens A LOT in the modern world.

Now you know the fundamental reason to have remarketing, let's talk about where you find your code in the first place. So what I've done is I've created an unlisted YouTube video only for the readers of this book. You can watch it at the link below and get free access to the video.

YouTube Video: **https://www.youtube.com/watch?v=d-IP6gQY78M**

As this process is quite a few steps it's much easier to watch a quick 2 minute video than trying to learn from all the advice in photos presented. So feel free to go and watch the video right now at the URL above. I would appreciate if you didn't share the video with people who haven't purchased this book. It would be much better to send them to Amazon, let them buy the book and then they'd get the video anyway.

On top of which, once you have your remarketing code, we go through in the video where to place your remarketing code on your site or landing page.

Once your account gets banned it becomes very difficult to get it unbanned which means you'd likely have to start the entire sandbox process again with a new account. No one wants that. So in the video you'll learn how to place the remarketing code on your Wordpress site and if you really don't want to do it yourself, 1. Ask your web guy to do it or if you don't have a web guy then someone on Fiverr will do it for you. Either way it's extremely simple to do.

Once you've done that, it's very important you set up a specific type of conversion code and action. What's a conversion code? Well I can tell you it's different from a remarketing code. They're most certainly not the same thing so don't treat them as the same. They both have different jobs so ensure right away you understand they're different.

So a conversion code simply allows you to track how many people have taken the desired action you want them to take on your site. For example the desired action for most business owners is they want new prospects to phone their office. That's one of the most effective uses of Adwords so to ensure you know how many people have called, we must set up a conversion code.

As this process is a few steps as well, I've set up another unlisted YouTube video right below where you can watch me take you through this step by step. After the video the entire process of conversion codes will be very very easy for you. You certainly won't have to guess around and waste countless hours figuring it out. Before you do watch the video, I've got something else related to conversion codes which is very important for you to be aware of.

It's not going to be a good idea for you to direct people to your office number right away. Now hold up a moment. That doesn't mean you don't want the calls forwarded to your office but instead you want people to call a number where you can track all of the calls coming through. This way you'll know how good your staff are on the phones (this shocks almost every business owner how poor their staff are at converting people to appointments).

So how do you go about sorting this out? 1. I'd strongly suggest going to Call Rail and signing up for their service. You get a 14 day free trial to see if you like the service which by the way you most certainly will and the support is really good there too.

Conversion Code YouTube Video
https://www.youtube.com/watch?v=EsiX0rtHYD8

Once you're in Call Rail as you can see below in figure 6.1, you simply click "Numbers" at the top of your screen and simply create a number for Adwords by following the simple instructions. Once you've done that you can now put the tracking number on your landing pages instead of your office so you can not only track the amount of conversions you're getting but also how good your staff are on the phones.

Remember, there's little point in focusing on click through rate and clicks if your ads themselves aren't converting. An ad which doesn't convert will only get you so far because conversions are all that matter. So if your ads aren't converting well then I'd recommend completely switching things up. It's too risky to be spending money on Google if you're getting little to show for it. So now you know.

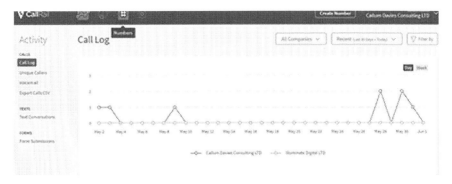

Figure 6.1 of the Call Rail homepage.

This may not have been the most glamorous chapter but it's certainly one of the most important you get this set up properly. The back end of your Google Adwords campaigns are so key and it puts you in a much better organisational position to change what doesn't work.

The best part is you're going to love the next chapter. When you learn how to research your competitors properly it becomes much easier to outperform every single one of them without huge amounts of work. Let's slide right into this.

Chapter 7

How a Ninja does Keyword Research

———— ♦ ————

R esearch. Research is the foundation of not only every Google Adwords campaign you run but also every advertising campaign you run altogether! The importance of you spending the time doing your research is absolutely critical. If you don't do this you leave yourself completely vulnerable to attack from competitors who will do the research.

As I've said many times before, it's one thing for a competitor to beat you by pure work ethic and strategy but a whole new thing if they beat you because you didn't take fundamental action. What makes it worse is 95% of businesses on Google don't do their research properly so as a result it becomes very difficult to craft campaigns and messages to fit their audience the best. Once you know what your competitors are doing well and what they're doing badly it becomes very easy to take advantage of all the work they've been doing.

What are all the Different Types of Keywords?

Let's start with keywords. Keywords are the holy grail of Google Adwords and knowing not only which keywords to use but also where to find these keywords is very important. So before we do any kind of research you must understand there's 3 types of keywords and this comes from Brad Geddes once again. Geddes suggests 3 types of keywords you want to use in Google which are:

1. Explicit Based Keywords e.g. *Plastic surgeon Los Angeles.*

2. Problem Based Keywords e.g. *How do I fix a leak in my basement?*

3. Symptom Based Keywords e.g. *Been in an accident?*

Let's break into each one of these in a bit more depth but first understand how a searcher conducts their Google search.

It's easy to fall into the trap of only using explicit based keywords I.e. ones with your city in them are the best because they're very specific to the location/s of your business. But remember not everyone conducts their search so rigidly. In many cases people search by simply asking a question into Google as shown in the above example or the type in a specific symptom of the problem they're experiencing.

Now that doesn't mean you shouldn't use explicit keywords as they have incredible value. It means you must not limit yourself to only explicit based keywords. Having more tools in your tool box is going to allow you to market much better than everyone else. You can't just rely on specific based keywords all the time which most of your competitors do.

First off, explicit based keywords go much deeper than simply having the city in the keyword. So let's start off with what explicit keywords are good for:

1. They're city specific meaning a person in or around your city searching for this type of keyword is going to be a person who is easily able to reach your business location in the first place.

2. They're relatively easy to find making it much easier for you to advertise on Google with quality keywords.

3. They generally have the most people searching for them than any other type of keyword which means you have a lot more traffic to work with.

The downsides:

1. As they're the most popular they're also the most competitive which means if you don't master copy which we'll explain later and master quality score it's going to be very difficult for you to rank in position 1.

2. They're also the most expensive keywords especially when in larger cities such as NYC, LA, Chicago, Houston etc which means it's easier to blow your budget.

3. They follow a rigid pattern which means plenty of great prospects who make great patients and clients for you don't search on them so you'd be missing out on other patients by focusing solely on these.

That's explicit based keywords. Overall they will form the forefront of your entire Google Adwords campaigns because you know a lot of people are searching for these keywords in the first place. The more people who are searching for these keywords the better because it gives you plenty of testing power. The more testing power you have at your disposal the faster you'll know what message and offer which work best with your audience.

Now as I mentioned before, take these keywords with the greatest caution if you don't want to overspend. You can set a limit on your account anyway but you don't want to reach your spending limit just off one keyword which you can easily do by the way especially if you're an personal injury attorney. So managing your budget on these keywords is going to be absolutely critical you don't lose control.

As you'll see later we'll be going through SEM Rush in a bit more depth but just so you know for now it's one of the easiest places to find explicit based keywords. It's much better than the Google Keyword Planner for this job and you can get a considerable amount of searches for free if you wanted. Now, what are you supposed to do in the situation if your city doesn't have enough searches for explicit based keywords? Well you have 3 options to choose from.

1. You focus on an explicit based keyword without the city I.e. *Auto Accident Chiropractor* as these keywords have a lot of searches despite being national keywords. Obviously city specific keywords are better but you can still laser target your audience with national keywords as well. By not having city specific keywords that doesn't mean you should ignore Google Adwords completely.

2. You either open up another practice in the main city you're near or you move your practice from your current location to a bigger city. You have much more opportunity in terms of potential patients you can acquire by doing this so it's an option for you to consider.

3. Focus more on problem based & symptom based keywords which we will talk about in just a moment.

So problem based keywords. Remember, people generally don't think very rigid when they have an urgent problem they want solving. They just want it solving.

People panic and the only thing they think to do is either how to fix the problem they're experiencing through some kind of question or type some of the symptoms they're experiencing into Google for a solution. Generally problem based keywords will not have a city attached to them because of how limited the searches are, unless a city like NYC or Los Angeles and even then the chances are slim of there being enough searches. So the mindset of each prospect will change depending on the buying stage they're at and this is the reason which makes problem based keywords so critical to Google Adwords success.

Generally when a person has typed in a explicit based keyword they're screening out to see who's the best they should go and see. They're interested in getting treatment or working with you on their case but it's not a super urgent problem they'd sell their house to solve. They just want information on who's position 1 and in their mind who's the best.

In addition, when people get distracted which they often do, the problem they're experiencing will get worse and when it gets worse the problem starts to become more and more urgent. It starts out as a little itch and escalates into a bleeding neck they want solved right away. So if you're not bidding on explicit based keywords then you're missing all these quality patients and cases who need your help RIGHT NOW.

Right now is key. Not tomorrow, not next year but NOW. These are the people who will pay the most money for your services and are also the patients and clients who become the most loyal because you helped them when they needed it most. Of course I'll show you later in this chapter how to find the best possible problem based keywords but understand for now their importance. Many businesses don't bid on them because they view them as unimportant. As they're national based keywords in their mind that means they're a complete waste of time. Obviously you know better.

Now, I'm not saying problem based keywords or even symptom based keywords are going to result in mass amounts of patients a month especially if you're in a smaller city. This is because they're national based keywords so it's difficult to know how many people in your city a month are searching for these keywords. What I'm saying is these keywords present you with a great opportunity to acquire very high quality patients right now. What's even better is most of your competitors ignore these keywords so the competition is much lower and sometimes there's no advertisers whatsoever in your city bidding on these keywords. This means you'll have little to no competition whatsoever so you'll have access to all the in need people who badly need your help.

Symptom based keywords. The final type of keyword you're going to want to use in your Adwords campaigns. Right away the advantages of symptom based keywords are:

1. Very cheap so your budget won't take much of a hit.

2. Very little competition as many of your competitors either don't know about these keywords or don't think they're worth the time to spend money on. This means you only have to advertise on these keywords with a good offer and you'll acquire more quality patients.

3. The prospect is at a very important stage of the buying cycle where they know they have a problem and are looking for a solution now.

<u>Disadvantages and drawbacks of symptom based keywords:</u>

1. They're harder to find and generally can be very obscure so will likely take much more time and effort to find them which is very similar to the effort required to find high quality problem based keywords.

2. The amount of searches per month are much less for your city than explicit based keywords alongside the fact there's no real accurate way of knowing how many searches a month there are on national based symptom keywords.

3. They're a little more time consuming in terms of crafting ad copy and you've got to be very careful you don't violate Google's terms of service when you're writing copy for these. The reason is because with explicit based keywords the copy can be very simple but with symptom and problem based keywords you're not following the same rigid keyword pattern.

So do these disadvantages mean I should just avoid symptom based keywords altogether? No of course not. It just means you must not base your entire advertising around these types of keywords because the main bulk of your new patients coming through from Adwords won't come from these keywords.

There's simply not enough searches in almost every city except NYC & Los Angeles. Either way symptom based keywords offer you a great advantage in the buying cycle because the person knows they have a problem. If a person doesn't believe they have a problem in the first place then they're not going to search for a solution. Why would they? They have no reason to if they think everything is okay.

This means these types of prospects are much more open to your solution right away rather than needing to think about it which no business owner likes to hear.

We want prospects to be able to move forward right away, not need more and more time to think about it which eventually leads to the dreaded no decision dynamic. Therefore you must not skip these keywords under any circumstances. Some of you may find you barely get any clicks on these keywords for the first 30-60 days. That's not the worst thing because you only pay Google when a person clicks on your ad so if no one clicks you don't have to pay. Your impressions are likely to be very low too and that's okay also. As long as you have a quality offer on symptom and problem based keywords you've put yourself in a great position to acquire very high quality patients. Ignore this advice at your peril.

So we've spoken heavily about the different types of keywords which is very important but that means nothing unless you know how to find these keywords in the first place. You know these quality keywords exist but don't have much clue of where to start looking. So let's discuss this right now.

Where Do I Find the Best Keywords?

To start with, I'd strongly recommend following the same process I'm about to layout for you. That doesn't mean you have to follow it step by step because you can tweak it and add anything else which you may find helpful. But I would recommend keeping all these steps in because of how important these sources of information are for high quality keywords you'll use in your Google Adwords campaigns.

1. Start with SEM Rush which you can see in figure 7.1 just below. This as I said before the fastest and easiest to find the best possible explicit based keywords for your campaigns.

You can see below this tool works in virtually any country and you can get a free 7 day trial if necessary. You don't have to pay for the tool if you don't want to. So, as you can see in Figure 7.1, the value in this tool is how easy it is to see the amount of times a keyword has been searched for and all the other quality explicit based keywords at the bottom you can use too. Sometimes it can be a little time consuming to think of all these possible keyword variations yet SEM Rush gives you plenty of options right at the bottom of the the service.

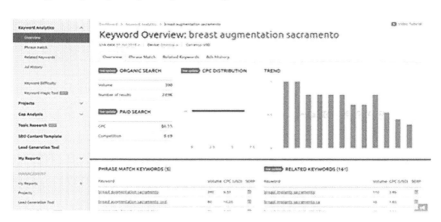

Figure 7.1 of a searched keyword in SEM Rush.

Now, I will say this. Sometimes when you type in one variation of an explicit based keyword I.e. *"Chicago Accident Lawyer"* and nothing comes up whatsoever including variations. Yet when you type in *"Accident Lawyer Chicago"* not only the keyword shows up but also plenty of variations too. So it can get a little frustrating when trying to find explicit based keywords and nothing comes up so make sure you exhaust every option before moving onto the national variations of these keywords. Even if a keyword option has only 10 searches a month it's still worth doing so don't ignore these.

2. Once you've collected all your explicit based keywords from SEM rush which I've said is the best tool for this, you'll want to go and start looking at the types of keywords your top competitors are using. To achieve this you'll want to use SpyFu which is another fantastic tool and only costs $30 a month and is one of the few tools you'll want to keep using month in and month out.

So how do we use this tool? Well as you can see in figure 7.2 right below, you'll want to type in your competitor's website URL and then click on the Adwords section. Once you've done that you'll want to click on PPC keywords and pay attention to the keywords they're using and the amount they're spending.

Figure 7.2 of an attorney's keywords in SpyFu.

This is a very important step because you're given all this valuable data about what you're competitors are doing right and what they're doing wrong. This type of data is data that's taken months for your competitor to build up to and you get it right in front of you for free to take advantage of. How fantastic is that?!

Often times you'll see your competitors bidding on standard explicit based keywords which is helpful for you to know but the best finds are the rare problem and symptom based keywords you may have not found yet. As I've said before these keywords offer you the greatest opportunity for finding the most loyal patients and clients you can find and you've barely had to do any work to find these keywords.

Now, some of you may say "Well if it's this easy what's stopping our competitors doing the exact same thing to us?". Great question. 1. Most competitors won't use SpyFu or any other tool well enough to find the different keywords you're bidding on & 2. Even if they did they'd struggle to match the offer and high standard of copy you'll learn to write from this book without serious long term training. So either way you have the upper hand. This leads perfectly into step 3 of studying your competitors copy.

3. You'll want to remain in SpyFu and click on the Ads tab in as you can see in figure 7.3 just below here. Now this is where things get very interesting. At this point you'll now know the types of offers your competitors are using which means you can start to craft out counter offers. When you know your competitors better than they know themselves it makes it much easier for you to create campaigns which counter and defeat their way of advertising on Google.

What you'll see as shown in figure 7.3 is the different pieces of copy being written too. What makes it even better for you is the copy from almost all of your competitors will be extremely bland and not have much fire to it meaning you won't have to spend so much time coming up with copy 100 times better. On top of which you'll also be able to pay attention to the amount a competitor is spending on Adwords.

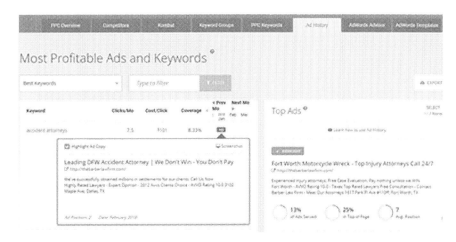

Figure 7.3 of an attorney's ads broken down in SpyFu.

When a competitor starts to lose the only fear based response they come up with is to raise their budget. Now that's all well and good but it fails when they're not in position 1 of Google because you're already spending less than them anyway and still outranking them so you only have to increase your budget a little bit more to keep outranking them.

You can quite literally with clickfraud technology and superior copy completely remove competitors from Google altogether because they simply can't compete with you. When a competitor has gotten to the point they can't compete with you then you're on the home straight.

The last thing you want to do here is see your competitors copy and then craft a slight improvement to their copy. The problem with this is you increase the chances of you fighting over scraps instead of dominating everyone being in position 1 whilst spending significantly less money than they're spending. So regardless of how bad your competitor's copy is, you must not take this as an excuse to craft slight improvement based copy. Ignore once again at your peril.

So understand you must not write any copy before you know your competitors copy inside and out. The last thing you want to do is spend all this effort crafting copy only to find out your competitor has already done the same thing.

4. The final step here of your keyword research is finding high quality problem based and symptom based keywords. Now as I already mentioned you'll find great examples in SpyFu of what some of your competitors are using. You can find great examples in SpyFu of the businesses like yours just in a different city too. However doing it only this way makes it harder for you to find keywords which you're competitors aren't bidding on. So let's dive into this.

As you can see below in figure 7.4 the picture of the Google keyword planner with a random example of a keyword we can use here. A word of warning, this method is going to not only be the most tedious but also take the most amount of time so if you aren't prepared to do this then you'll not only miss out on quality patients but also leave your competitors to take these patients off you and establish a stronger hold of the market. So you've been warned.

Either way you want to start with just by typing in problems and symptoms which come to mind people would have who are considering your type of service. You as a business owner will know these problems and symptoms better than any advertising agency unless the agency undergoes rigorous research on your market which they rarely do anyway.

Figure 7.4 of a child custody keyword example in the Google Keyword Planner.

Once you've typed in one problem based or symptom based keyword, start looking down at all the potential variations you can use. Often when you type something in to get started you'll get much better keywords on variation which will help you even more. Then you can start to build ad groups of keywords which we'll go through in a later chapter in much more depth. Now this process is a little tedious yes but this is one of the most important ways to find rare keywords you can use for your business.

Seriously I'd recommend not taking this information in this chapter lightly. When you start to goldmine for these golden keywords, you'll be so surprised at how many patients you were missing out on simply by not finding these keywords. It's actually terrifying how many patients you can miss out on. Recently I showed a client down in Dallas Texas how his cosmetic surgery was missing out on more than 30 new patients a month on these problem and symptom based keywords. His competitors weren't even getting these patients either on these keywords! The potential here is enormous for success when you know what you're doing.

You won't want to miss this next chapter. You'll find out exactly what will happen if you fail to not only do competitive research but also fail to do it properly. Get ready, you'll be shocked at what you hear!

Chapter 8

Only Losers Fail to
do Competitive Research

———◆———

Now this is a short chapter especially compared to my previous chapters. However, this is very important. If you fail to research your competitors properly you're in for serious trouble. By serious trouble I mean thousands of dollars wasted on advertising and to top it all off the potential of you going out of business.

Yes, competitive research is that critical to do. Even if you as the business owner don't want to do it yourself you must make sure you hire someone who does it to the level I've described in the previous chapter. So listen up, you could lose your business if you fail to listen to the importance of competitive research.

What Happens if I FAIL to Do Competitive Research?

As I mentioned before, you must have researched your competitors previous ads which didn't work and their ads which they're currently running. The reason this data is so critically important is because you already have knowledge now of what is working and what isn't.

Why is this important? Well it saves you at least 2-4 weeks of testing to find out what works depending on your market and can save you at least $1,000 on testing and gives you a great starting point. Honestly, no one likes to start from scratch if they can get a head start. If you can start in first position on the track over last position, almost every single one of you would start in first position. So what's the point in failing to do competitive research and starting in last position?

As a result, any business who simply refuses to do competitive research is happy starting in last position. Most of you will agree time is extremely important so why waste at least 2-4 weeks of testing when you already have a strong idea of what's working for your competitors. Be smarter. Don't take the long way round if you don't have to.

Now some of you will say you want your ads to be very unique and don't want to copy competitors. To that I will quote the great Pablo Picasso who said "Good artists copy, great artists steal". So I'm not saying outright copy exactly what your competitors are doing and hope for the best. I'm saying use what they've done as a blueprint of where to start and craft your own message from there.

For example, your competitors may be using specific types of words which are working great I.e. Using the phrase "Are you tired" instead of "Are you exhausted" will save you much time knowing this. Now you can weave this into your current unique value you offer and then go from there. It's not rocket science. It just has to be done properly so you extract as much data from what your competitors are doing with Adwords.

Now, I said something very bold at the start of the chapter. I said if you didn't do competitive research either at all or not very well then there would be a higher chance of you going out of business. I didn't say it was a guarantee, I said you increase the chance of that happening. The reason I said this is because the market is changing all the time and a competitor of yours may be very good at anticipating what they need to solve next in the market.

If you're not aware of this many of your current customers who've worked with for years can easily transfer over to your competitor because they have a better solution. If a competitor has a better solution to a person's problem then your current customers are going to be at least intrigued. On top of which you're doing your current customers a disservice if you're not keeping up with the market because you're not providing them the best possible solution.

It's very surprising how easily you can take your eye off the ball. You focus so much on helping your patients and clients you end up forgetting your competitors are taking over the market on Google. Sorry to disappoint you, you've either got to keep your eye on this ball or hire an expert to do it for you.

I'll give you a great example. Blockbuster used to be the most popular store you'd go to for new videos, movies and video games to rent out. As blockbuster stopped paying attention Netflix came in and Reed Hastings (Founder of Netflix) saw how the market was changing to watching movies online. Less people wanted to leave the comfort of their own homes. They just wanted an easier way to watch movies and TV Shows. Netflix came in and wiped Blockbuster out. Now I know this seems like a rare story but it happens everyday. You just don't see it happening.

So once you have your eyes on exactly what your competitors are doing it's then much easier for you to create solutions for existing and new customers which are better than everyone else's. This way your competitors customers have potential to come over to you instead of you losing customers to them. Much better scenario right? So let's push towards it.

Study the previous chapter and this one in more depth. Once you know the material you can hire or get one of your employees to do this kind of work for you. If you do this then you'll be one step closer to completely dominating your city. You're providing the best solution and you're providing it to more people. It's a win win.

The next chapter we're going to dive into constructing your offer. We're going to dispel myths of what most people think an offer is and ensure your offer is the only offer to people suffering from a specific problem you solve. Let's do that now!

Chapter 9

Putting Together the Perfect Cake a.k.a. Creating Your Offer for Google Adwords

———◆———

An offer. It's all about the offer. All online advertising comes down to how good of an offer you can create. Seriously, a good or a bad offer can make or break your online advertising. Now of course this book is specifically about success with Google Adwords but the good news is a lot of these principles can be applied to any other online advertising method such as Facebook Lead Generation, Instagram, Snapchat etc. Don't feel these methods can only be used for Google. There's no need to limit yourself when there are so many options for these strategies.

The Truth Behind What an Offer REALLY is

So let's start with the most basic information, what is an offer? It's a simple question and one which most business owners feel they know the answer to. What I can say is almost no business owner or digital agency has any idea of what an offer really is. It's quite scary when you think how easy it is to understand what an offer really is, start applying it and immediately start seeing results. Understand, an offer is NOT what you're selling. I'm going to repeat that again. An offer is NOT what you're selling. Yes you heard my twice and my answer was the same both times.

In reality, an offer to quote David Garkfinkel in his book "Breakthrough Copywriting" is: "An offer is what a person can do with what you are selling, all of the components, the big picture of your product, service or information product". So what does this mean? Well for starters it means an offer goes way beyond just what you're selling. If you sell Rhinoplasty then that isn't an offer. If you're a personal injury attorney then personal injury representation is not an offer either. Once you've understood this, let's go deeper.

So start to think, what can a person do with what you're selling? For example, a cosmetic dentist or orthodontist selling Invisalign might say, you have a better chance of making a great first impression, being the envy of your friends, getting more job interviews etc. How much better does that sound than simply saying, Invisalign will straighten your teeth. I'm not saying having straight teeth isn't important but what I'm saying is there are much bigger benefits to a person having straight teeth will OFFER them.

Many of you may not have gone through this process before and that's okay. Most agencies don't take you through this process. It's key to start by taking your service and right away thinking, what can a person do with my service? Then to differentiate yourself, what can a person do with my service they can't do with a competitors? It's really simple when you start following this process to acquire more patients and clients because it's easier for people to see what they get from your service.

Now going deeper into constructing an offer. Don't worry, I will number the entire process out for creating your own offer so you don't waste time figuring out where to start. So understand, if you just describe in more detail what you're selling I.e. for a cosmetic surgeon you describe how the process of Breast Augmentation works, then once again you haven't made an offer. One thing I see time and time again is on a business owner's website, they've just described the service and haven't made an offer at the end for the person to act on. You can't expect people to call you if you haven't made a proper offer. Remember, people care about themselves the most. The good news is when you craft your offer to what the person wants it becomes very easy to increase your calls and enquires.

Now, an offer isn't just what a person can do with your product or service but also what the service can do for them. People don't like to feel they have to do a lot of work. They want things handed to them on a plate with minimal effort required. So cosmetic surgery might improve a woman's ability to attract a better partner into her life. See what I did? I showed what cosmetic surgery could do for a woman, not what she would have to do.

On top of which, I described the woman in action. I didn't say she could sit at home and men would come to her. I said she could go out and attract a better partner. What this does is it allows the person to imagine themselves in the same situation as you've described because of movement you've created. For example, if a car is parked and isn't moving you almost instantly lose focus. But when a car is racing and moving fast you eyes immediately pay attention. That's the power of movement over being static.

Understand, your offer is your solution to your patient's problems. Your solution is the main reason people are interested in giving you a call. Of course status helps but a person with no status and a great solution can attract more patients than a person with status and a bad offer. This is because an offer tells the person what the person gets and how their problem will be solved. A bad offer just describes the service. A person can't really imagine the service you've described. It's boring. There's no life to it. A person can't visualise what they get and all they care about is their problems being solved.

This is the sole reason many clients who signed with me over a very large agency with 50+ employees. They much preferred my customised offer to solve their specific problem than what any other agency had proposed. Like I said, when you can show people how easily your offer solves their problem they'll be lining up in queues wanting to work with you.

Some of you at this point will probably be thinking, I'm limited on characters on Google Adwords so I can't construct an offer like this. Don't worry, we'll be going into that later in this chapter. But remember, the good news is you can apply creating a fantastic offer to any advertising method. Doesn't matter what it is, you need a great offer. Plain and simple. The only change is how you present the offer which we'll get to later in this chapter.

How to Construct a High Quality Offer for Your Campaigns

Quickly, let's outline the process of creating a good offer:

1. What service do you want to advertise?

2. What problem does your ideal patient/client want solving your service can solve?

3. What does your ideal patient/client really not want to lose in their current situation I.e. For a divorce attorney a person likely won't want to lose their children in a custody battle?

4. What tangible benefits I.e. Getting a new job can a person get from receiving your service?

5. What are the intangible benefits I.e. More confidence a person can get from receiving your service?

6. What can the person do with your service?

7. What can your service do for them?

8. How can the person get access to your offer I.e. Have to call the front desk etc?

9. What does your offer cost? (This is something you won't reveal until the consultation unless a low tripwire offer I.e. $37.

10. What bonuses can you offer to better solve your potential patient/client's problem & make your offer more valuable in the process i.e. Free product you have etc.

So you can follow this process every single time you want to create an offer for each individual service you offer and/or want to advertise too. Now, for Adwords we've got to present our offer slightly differently because you're limited on characters. It's the same with any advertising method e.g. A billboard you only have limited space to create a good claim.

We will go in much greater depth in chapter 16 on copy later but understand this first: You have 2 headlines both limited to 30 characters each and a smaller space for text limited to 90 characters. You simply can't write lots of text so it means you must adapt. Those who thrive aren't the strongest businesses but the businesses which are the most adaptable.

As a result, the easiest formula to follow for Adwords is by stating the biggest tangible benefit a person can get whilst not having to do something they hate I.e. **"Win your case 40% faster without any money down!"**.

What have I done there? I've stated part of our offer is we win quickly and the client doesn't have to risk putting any money down in the first place. How much better does that sound than: **"30 years of experience. Call for your free consultation today!"**.

The difference is pretty strong. Now I'm going to mention this briefly here but it's importance cannot be denied. The first part of your first headline has to be the keyword you're bidding on I.e. If you're bidding on *"NYC Breast Augmentation"* then that must be in your first headline. If you don't put this Google will drop your relevance meaning it's very unlikely your ads will rank high enough to have the impact you want. So don't take this lightly.

Once that's done, your second headline can be used for the first part of your benefit I.e. **Improve Your Nose. Call Us Today**. (This would be for Rhinoplasty). Now, you have your Ad extensions too which must be used for Tangible & Intangible benefits the person will get from your service. At this point you've said very little about who you as a business and instead offered specific tangible and intangible benefits the person wants and told them exactly how to get these benefits. Are you starting to see how this approach is much better than talking about how good your practice is and how long you've been in business…?

Finally, you can describe your offer in a bit more detail on your landing page. Once again we'll go much more in depth on this in chapter 18 but understand this still isn't the place to write lots of words. You want to summarise your offer I.e. *Tangible & intangible benefits* the person gets, *what they don't lose* from working with you and *exactly how to get started*. You give some testimonials of current patients and clients and give a little more detail of the service itself. That's it. Don't worry if this sounds a little unclear, you'll get a much clearer picture when we go in more depth on structure and strategy behind landing pages for Google Adwords.

Get ready, the next chapter you're going to start learning how to set up your campaigns properly. You're in a great position having all the foundations right to then be able to launch campaigns as quickly & effectively as possible.

Chapter 10

Boldly launching
your Campaigns

———————◆———————

Wow we've come far. Now at this point in the past 9 chapters all of the foundations have been set up properly for you to launch your campaigns. Remember, if you haven't set the foundations up properly, then your campaigns won't do nearly as well as they should do. So don't skip the foundations.

I encourage you to read this chapter and to the end of this book and once you're done and then go back through the first 9 chapters and study the foundations once again. I cannot stress how important these first 9 chapters are to your Adwords success. I know they're a little tedious and boring because you want to jump right into action and start advertising.

Imagine if a cosmetic surgeon didn't plan your facelift and just went right in with no planning. Just imagine how you'd feel. Pretty terrified right? So your failure to set up the foundations properly can kill your entire campaign.

Let's start with campaign set up. Remember there are 3 levels to every single campaign which are:

1. The campaign level I.e. You'll set up targeting ad scheduling etc.

2. The ad group level I.e. You'll organise your ads and keywords into their own specific groups.

3. The ad level I.e. You'll just manage your ads on this level.

We're starting in the campaign level because it's important you understand the different options and which ones will best benefit you. There's lots of options and each one has a different purpose. Most business owners will start on "All Features" as you can see in figure 10.1 and will also start with just the "Search Network" also made clear in figure 10.1.

DO NOT START WITH BOTH THE DISPLAY & SEARCH NETWORK. Again you want your ads as focused as humanly possible on your specific goal. When you choose both networks you aren't optimising either platform so you end up getting 50/50. Bottom line is to start with the search network and then later on use the display network to scale out your campaigns. Of course the display network is a completely different animal in it's own right but for now understand, start with the search network only.

Figure 10.1 showing the page when you start a campaign.

As you can see in figure 10.2, you want to have search partners selected to increase your chances of more traffic. Most businesses in cities of less than 200,000 population are going to be limited on traffic anyway depending on the niche so it's very important you get as much traffic as Google will allow you. For this chapter this is all you need to know.

The next 2 chapters will be even more critical for you because we're diving into targeting and how to bid properly so you don't blow your budget. Always remember, the right offer in front of the wrong people will never work. So let's jump into the next chapter right now.

Figure 10.2 showing Google "Search Partners" selected for your campaign.

Chapter 11

Laser Your Targeting
to find Wally

———————◆•————————

Targeting besides copy are the 2 things you must get right. If you don't get these right then you've got no chance to succeed with Google Adwords. Remember, the greatest offer in the world doesn't mean anything if it's put in front of the wrong people. How useful is it selling a Golden State Warrior's shirt in front of an audience of Cleveland Cavalier fans…?

Very few people would buy. You may've found a hungry market but it's the wrong hungry market for what you have to sell. In the context of local businesses, the biggest targeting errors people make is showing their ads too far out of where patients and clients will come and do business with them. It's a very easy mistake to make and an extremely costly one if not dealt with.

The World's Best Mindset for Google Adwords Targeting

Let's quickly talk mindset before we go deeper into this. Local business targeting, keyword selection etc is completely different to national targeting. You're not a national business, you're a local business. So if you decide to further your learning outside of this book to other sources make sure you understand the difference between local business Adwords & national business Adwords. Both are very different so it's important you don't view them as the same because they're not. They're plain and simply not. Now that's cleared up let's go deeper into targeting.

Location Targeting for Local Businesses

As you can see in figure 11.1 the targeting option itself on the first page in Adwords when you decide to create your own campaigns. You've got multiple options here so pay attention. The first 3 options are only really relevant to national based businesses and as we've already established, you're a local business. So always start with the option "Let me choose" and go from there.

Figure 11.1 showing different location options in Google Adwords targeting.

Once you've done that, click on "Advanced Search" to bring up more options. Yes you get given a lot of options when you first see this but don't worry it's really very simple. Just follow my instructions and you'll do great. Now, as you can see in figure 11.2, you'll want to click on "Radius Targeting" which allows you to laser focus on a specific mile radius around your practice. This is extremely important because many of you either have 1 location or multiple locations and people generally won't travel more than 30 miles to come see you.

The only exception to this rule is attorneys as they work with people all across the state so they can simply type in just the city they work in. For everyone else, we must follow the radius targeting rule. What's point in advertising to people who can't even come in and visit you…?

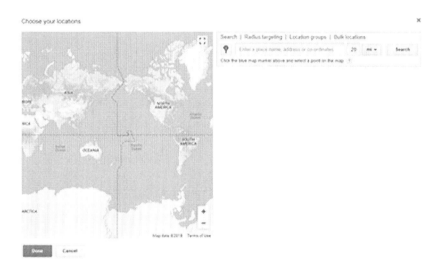

Figure 11.2 of Radius targeting.

I remember when I first started doing online advertising and I made the catastrophic mistake of doing 40 miles out for a client. One day the client ended up getting a new patient who had quite literally travelled 40 miles to come and work with the client. Now that tells you the power of a fantastic offer targeted to the right people but, I wouldn't recommend doing this. It's too much of a risk to target people beyond the vicinity of your practice.

Now, some of you may argue you're going to be really limited on the amount of people you can target if you reduce your radius. Now that may be true but would you rather have less people to target who are able to spend money with you or more people to target who have a much lower chance of working with you? I bet most of you chose the latter. As I said before, we're laser targeting the best potential patients and clients for your business in order to maximise ROI. I could just say target everyone in your city but you end up spending at least 3 times more than you needed to acquire a lesser result. What business owner wants that…?

Now, copy and paste the address of your practice location then click add. If you have multiple locations in the same city then simply copy and paste the location of each practice and click "Add" each time.

How Do I Go About Selecting Specific Suburbs & Excluding Specific City Areas?

So once you've done that you'll be able to see in figure 11.3 the options of "Add", "Exclude" & "Nearby". Many of you will know your location very well and at this point know where your best patients and clients come from. So I'd recommend clicking on exclude on specific zip codes and locations if you haven't had great experience in acquiring patients and clients from that area. Of course you can test it but I would recommend excluding a specific area once you've found out in your data it isn't converting very well. (We'll discuss data later).

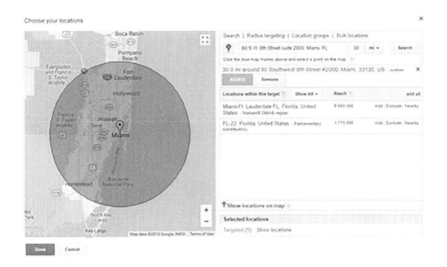

Figure 11.3 showing adding, excluding and nearby options in Adwords targeting.

The "Nearby" tab is very important too if you want to expand your targeting as much as possible. For many of you simply starting with just the zip code of your practice will be enough at this stage. For others who know for a fact there are specific locations around your practice/s which convert better than others then feel free to click "Nearby" and include those also.

One thing I will say is if you don't have a laser targeted knowledge of where your patients come from then start learning fast. The faster you have access to this knowledge the faster you can start crafting quality offers to reach these types of people. As you know, the better the location and people you target the better your offer will come across EVEN if it's an average offer. (That's not an excuse to craft an average offer though).

So this is the area where most campaigns get screwed up. Seriously I cannot tell you the amount of business owners who haven't had their agencies set this up right. You have 3 options of who you want to see your ads and and who you want to exclude from seeing your ads. This goes beyond just location based targeting.

Understand, the only people you want seeing your ads are the people searching for what you offer who are located in your city or very close to it. The only time this differs if you're a national attorney or a world renown medical practice and even then you'd want to separate your campaigns based on each location.

How do most agencies and businesses screw up here? Well as you can see from figure 11.4, they allow people outside of their city and location to be able to see their ads also.

How Do I Ensure my Ads are Only Shown to Those in my Area?

Now of course people outside your location search for what you have to offer all the time but that doesn't mean you want your ads shown to them. If people are considering moving to your area and want your services then it's better if they see your SEO ranking because you don't pay any money to be shown there. However direct response marketing is all about getting people who are in a position to take action to call you right now. Otherwise you're just spending money on building awareness and Google Adwords' purpose is not to build awareness.

Therefore you want to make sure you see in figure 11.4 below you only include people in your city and your exclude people outside your city. That way the only people who see your ads are people who want your offer and are in a nearby location where they can redeem your offer.

As I said before, that mistake can cost you at least $3,000 extra a month minimum. What value is it for people to be in Austin and click on your ads if your business is based in Miami…? It's of no value to you at all because these people aren't in a position to take advantage of your offer which means you've wasted a click for nothing. The whole reason we're able to acquire such a high ROI in the first place is by maximising every single click. Not by maximising every 3rd click, but every single click. When you do this you start to make a much greater return off every single click rather than making a return off your entire ad budget. It's much more focused and will make you much more money doing it this way.

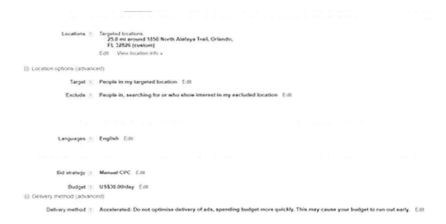

Figure 11.4 showing what location you want to allow your ads to be shown to.

Make sure you double check before you launch any campaign this is set up properly. Once you've done that you can sleep much easier at night. Next chapter we're going to jump face first into how to bid correctly on every single keyword and ad group you decide to run ads on. There's lots of different options which leads to lots of confusion so let's dispel this confusion right now.

Chapter 12

Blow your Budget
or Blow Up Your Competitors

———— ◆ ————

Bidding. Oh how this is important. It's not as simple to know the amount you want to bid for each keyword and then bidding exactly that. There's a lot more which goes into bidding successfully you might not know hence the importance of this chapter.

Therefore right away it's important you remove the mindset of seeing the cost of a keyword, bidding that exact cost and then it'll automatically turn into results because that's too straightforward. I'm all for making things nice and easy but I'm against making things a lot simpler than they actually are.

Optimal Bidding via Ad Groups

Now as you can see in figure 12.1 the 8 different bidding strategies which you can start with. Now regardless of the state of your ad account meaning if you're brand new to this or you've advertised out of your account before, you'll want to start with "Manual CPC" bidding. Yes you heard me right. Even if you've got at least 30 converted actions on your account I.e. 30 calls you'll still want to start by manually bidding via CPC. Why have I suggested this…?

I've suggested it because in the very beginning it's very important for local businesses to manage their budget effectively to ensure you can keep investing into Adwords. If you blow your budget in 30 days you're going to be very reluctant to try again which would be fair enough.

Therefore it's absolutely critical you manage your budget effectively which manual CPC bidding allows you to do. Some of you may argue you'll want to start on "Maximise conversions" which is a fair assertion. The issue with that in the beginning is you don't want to destroy your budget so once you have a fantastic idea of what you need to bid to see consistent success and you've achieved at least 30 conversions, then you can start to bid via conversions. However until you've done that it's going to be much better for you to only start with "Manual CPC".

Figure 12.1 showing the different bidding options in Google Adwords.

Now what the heck are you supposed to even start bidding? Well as you can see in figure 12.2 where you'll set your budget amount, you'll start by giving an entire budget for the whole campaign. This is important because you have a good idea of how much you have available to invest and using your goals know how much you'll want to achieve out of the initial budget you set.

So easiest way to start is by bidding 20% above what you know your budget to be. The reason I say this is because you don't want to have any complications where you find yourself having to bid more than you need to. You want to start high right off the bat and then your high quality score will bring your bids right back down again so you'll pay less than anticipated. That's a much better scenario than finding out your ads aren't really getting any traction and you now have to bid much more than you initially thought. So when in doubt start 20% above what your budget is. Don't be scared either. You'll rarely pay this much anyway and if you're really scared then you can set a cap on the amount of money you'll spend before your ads stop showing e.g. set a cap for $150.

Figure 12.2 showing where to set your daily budget.

Now you're ready to start bidding via your ad group which has it's own separate chapter in it's own right. What you need to know for now is the keywords you decide to bid on will need to be organised into an ad group I.e. You bid on personal injury attorney Chicago and your ad group would be personal injury attorney Chicago.

Once you've done this you can start adding in variations to the ad group such as Chicago personal injury attorney etc. This is where your bids will become much more specific as to how much you'll be spending. Therefore it's critical you know the price of each keyword you decide to go after and make a 20% increase right away to ensure your campaigns hit off with a bang. The last thing you want as I've already said is for your campaigns to come out of the gates slowly. You lose all your momentum and if anything Google don't prioritise you nearly as much. Now that isn't factual but it's come from my observation having come out of the blocks too slowly before. So you've been warned.

How Do I Best Bid Via Desktop, Mobile & Individual Keywords?

Now this is where things get very interesting. Most people have no idea this option even exists partly because it's much harder to find than in Facebook. Of course I'm talking about bidding via Mobile & Desktop. With Facebook, the option to show your ads only on mobile and desktop is right infront of you whereas for Google Adwords you've got to really hunt to find it. But for your pleasure, you'll know how to find it and use it properly simply by following what I'm about to tell you. Just quickly though, you don't want to solely bid on Mobile or Desktop with Google Adwords like you would with Facebook. Most people nowadays are almost always on their phones when using Facebook which means it can be ineffective to run campaigns to the desktop on Facebook.

Adwords however is different. Currently it's about 70-30 of mobile users to desktop using and searching through Google Adwords. What does this mean? Well it means desktop isn't totally worthless and as a result you'll want to bid to suit both mobile and desktop users. Remember, mobile is still the priority so when we go in depth on landing pages you'll realise why we're prioritising our landing pages for the mobile phone. So to start with, go into your campaign menu and at the top of the screen as you can see in figure 12.3, click on the edit button next to where it says budget. Once you're there, you'll see in figure 12.4 where it says "Change devices bid adjustment" so click that. Now you'll have 3 different options to determine your bid adjustment:

Figure 12.3 showing how to access the option to adjust your device bid.

Figure 12.4 showing how to configure your mobile and desktop bids.

1. Mobile phones i.e. iphones, Android, Microsoft phones etc.

2. Desktop computers i.e. Laptops, Mac book pros, Chrome Books etc.

3. Tablets i.e. ipads, Kindles etc.

Remember, when you first start your campaigns, Google will naturally start both mobile & desktop off at 50-50 so as you can see in figure 12.4 you'll want to click "Bid adjustment".

Once there you can increase the budget of mobile phones to 20% and decrease desktop by 30% leaving tablets the same. Simply because mobile phones are the easiest to access and carry around it means more searches come in from them. Tablets still have value but remember, *people can't call your office from a tablet* which is the whole purpose of a local business using Adwords in the first place. Facebook is the place where you collect leads and then call them back. With Adwords, we want the caller to call in right away because they have a specific problem they want solved because they're searching for the solution in the first place!

Figure 12.5 showing how to bid via the ad group level.

Adjusting Your Bids as Your Campaign Progresses

I told you this chapter would be a longer one! Now we've diving into making bid adjustments as your campaign progresses. Remember we won't just keep the campaign at the same bid amount the entire time. This does nothing because what happens when we want more patients and want to start showing our ads more often to attract more people in? Exactly! So the easiest way to adjust your bids as you can see in figure 12.5 is to bid via the ad group level and adjust for the first 2 weeks.

Once you've reached the 2 week mark, I'd recommend as you can see in figure 12.6 to start bidding via keywords because at this point you've found keywords which don't convert very well. Therefore you'll want to start turning these keywords off because they're not working for you and you're taking traffic away from the keywords which are working.

Now all you'll do is either increase or decrease your budget on each keyword depending on how well it's converting. If it's converting well then the logical thing to do would be to double down on it. If it's converting but not doing that great then you can decrease the bid because you don't want to miss out on quality patients and clients converting. If the keyword plain and simply isn't doing much for you except driving up your budget then turn it off. Just one more thing to do with adjusting your bids, make sure you increase by 10-30%. Don't go beyond 30% because you don't want to pay more than necessary but don't go less than 10% otherwise your increased bids may not have any impact at all.

Figure 12.6 showing how to change your keyword bids.

How to Accelerate Your Results with Accelerated Bidding

Finally we can talk about accelerated bidding. Figure 12.7 shows you the feature of accelerated bidding and how to turn it on. Many industry leaders will disagree with me here and suggest you'll just want to go normal bidding. The reason I don't agree with that is because you want information as quickly as possible with a local business campaign and the faster you know what works and what doesn't the faster you can progress. This is one of the reasons many businesses are told they won't see results until 90-120 days in. The agency they're working with doesn't spend fast enough which means it takes 5 times as long to get the same data in you would've got had you done accelerated bidding.

On top of which, you only pay if someone clicks on your ad so if someone doesn't click it doesn't matter how many people Google shows your ads to because your budget isn't increasing. So don't worry about this at all. Understand we want data as quickly as possible to ensure we make the right changes to acquire high quality patients and clients as fast as possible. As the great John Wooden said, "Be quick but not in a hurry".

Figure 12.7 showing how to change your bidding to accelerated bidding.

Woah, we're done with this chapter. Yes it was quite dense but very important. It takes away the assumption you can just bid on keywords and do well. It may start this way but it certainly won't end that way. Next we're diving right into ad extensions and exactly how to optimise them so they don't completely flop on your campaigns. Let's go!

Chapter 13

Extend your Ads
to Ensure Safety

———◆———

This is a topic where again a lot of businesses and agencies don't set up properly. As we'll mention later in the copy chapter, ad extensions are just an extension on your ad which allow you to write whatever you like about your business You must write powerful descriptive words of the page you want to send people too I.e. Relieve Painful Headache instead of just free consultation.

I'm not saying you can't have free consultation as part of an ad extension but make sure your ad extensions aren't plain and boring. You're limited as it is with your headline and ad copy so the last thing you want to do is waste the characters you're given on your ad extensions. *Understand, every word you use must communicate you can solve the person's biggest problem.*

Most people just see ad extensions as extra writing instead of a bigger opportunity to communicate with their audience how they can solve their problem. So now you have this fundamental mindset, let's dive into the different types of ad extensions first. So what are ad extensions in the first place? Ad extensions as you'll see in each image in this chapter are extra pieces of information which go below your copy. Ad extensions simply contribute to the copy and headline you've written in the first place. Ad extensions do not make the entire ad but they do compliment your ad. So understand, the businesses who use ad extensions will have far more people clicking their ads than those who don't use ad extensions. Either way they're important to having success on Adwords. So let's dive into each ad extension and the purpose of each extension.

Call Extensions

Let's start with the call extension. As a local business this is arguably besides the location extension going to be the most important. If you decide hire an agency who's lazy then make sure they at least set up the call extension and location extension. What's a call extension? Simply put, it's the number you want potential patients and clients to call to book their appointment. Remember this is very important because 70-80% of all your enquiries will come from the mobile phone. On top of which the call extension is the easiest way for a person to actually contact your business on Adwords because it's right in front of them as you can see in figure 13.1. The person doesn't have to click the number on your landing page and instead can just click one button on your ad and then they ring your office. It's really that simple.

Figure 13.1 showing a call extension.

Now some of you may be thinking well how do I set up a call extension? Well fortunately for you it's very simple. You create all your ad extensions in the same place and don't worry, I'll walk you through how to set up each ad extension so you don't have to mess around trying to figure this out for yourself. So for all ad extensions as you can see in figure 13.2:

1. Go to the bottom of the page in creating a new campaign.

2. You'll see all the different ad extensions you can choose right in front of you.

3. Simply click the one you want to work on and then go from there. (You can follow this formula for every single ad extension).

Figure 13.2 showing how to find ad extensions in your Google Adwords campaign.

To set up your call extension, you click on the call extension at the bottom of the page as you can see in figure 13.2, then you'll want to click new number. From there as you'll be able to see in figure 13.3, all you have to do is type in the number you want shown. Now, I will recommend creating some kind of tracking number for this because it makes it much easier for you to track the number of calls, quality of calls etc which you can use in Call Rail. That way people call your tracking number which is routed to the front desk of your office. Really simple and once it's set up it makes life so much easier for you to determine the quality of people giving you a call in the first place.

Figure 13.3 showing where to type in your tracking number.

Location Extensions

Location extensions as I mentioned alongside call extensions are the 2 most important for any local business advertising on Google. Never ignore these. All the location extension does as you can see in figure 13.4 is simply shows the specific address of where your practice/s or firm/s are located. That way it makes it very easy for potential patients and clients to know exactly where you are. No guessing on their part whatsoever and as a result you reduce the uncertainty in your prospect's mind of where they have to travel to get their problem solved. It may not seem important on the outside but on the inside this is incredibly important.

Pacin Levine | Aggressive Injury Attorney
(Ad) www.pi-law.com/ ▾ +1 800-247-2727
Injured? Accident? Slip and Fall? Available 24/7. Free Consultation.
♀ 1150 NW 72nd Ave #600, Miami, FL - Open today · Open 24 hours ▾

Figure 13.4 showing a location extension on a Google ad.

Even more interesting is how do you set up your location extension? This one is the only ad extension you have to leave Google to finalise. Your email you set up your Adwords account must be the same email connected to your Google My Business account and for anyone who doesn't know what a Google my business account is or GMB for short is simply your business being listed as a business on Google in the first place. If you don't have a GMB account then go and make one. It's really simple and easy to do.

Once you've done this, your Ad account and GMB account must be both connected to your email address which I recommend using a GMAIL address for. Now you've done that as you can see in figure 13.5, your GMB will come up so you can link it as a location extension. Remember, if you're inviting a person to work on your ad account make sure you've also invited them to your GMB account as well otherwise they can't do the location extension for you. Which as I've already stated isn't something you want to miss out on.

Use locations from Google My Business

If you'd like to use all locations from the Google My Business account you selected, skip this step.

When you add a filter, only locations that meet its conditions will be imported into AdWords. For example, you can import only locations with a certain business name or within a particular category. Learn more

Business name ▾ is [ ] ✕

+ AND

Done   Cancel

Figure 13.5 showing you where to link your GMB account to your Google Adwords.

Sitelink Extensions

Sitelinks are very important also. As you've seen from figure 13.2 on the previous pages, sitelinks are ranked as 2nd on your choice of ad extensions. This is the ad extension where you get the chance to write the most about your business of all the ad extensions you're given.

What even is a sitelink extension? A sitelink extension is a clickable extension as you can see below in figure 13.6 which allows prospects to go to a separate page on your website for different information. For example if you're advertising for auto accidents you may decide to have a sitelink which takes people to specific information on your website about dealing with an auto accident. All you're doing is giving people the opportunity to find more information about what you're advertising.

Dental Implant Center | Serving Tanglewood, River Oaks
[Ad] www.bellaireoralsurgery.com/ ▾
What are dental implants and your tooth replacement options? Learn more now!
Easy Care Routine · Increased Confidence · Improved Chewing Ability
Contact Us · Dr. Iero · Other Services · About our Practice
♀ 6800 West Loop S, Bellaire, TX · Open today · 8:00 am – 2:00 pm ▾

Figure 13.6 showing you what sitelinks look like on a Google ad.

The set up of this may sound counter intuitive and may go against what you've learned before. So with sitelinks the way Google wants you to use them is by having 4 different links to different pages on your site I.e. contact us page, auto accident page, testimonials page etc.

However the problem with this is it doesn't support our main objective of converting traffic from Google in the first place. The reason for this is because if you send people to pages on your site which for the most part aren't optimised a person will likely read your information and then leave. You've just paid money for a person to click your ad and then leave without taking any action. This is something you want to avoid as it doesn't support your best interests. So instead you're going to create 4 separate links of the same landing page so every single sitelink you have just goes to the landing page you want. This way if someone wants to click on testimonials then they'll see all the testimonials on the landing page you've designed.

Just so you know this isn't difficult to do. All you have to do is go into your website or landing page software where the landing page is located and duplicate the landing page an extra 4 times so you have 5 versions of your landing page all identical. Now as you can see in figure 13.7 you simply copy and paste the link into the URL section of each variation of the page. Once you've done this you can create a mini headline and description too. Once again, if you're doing testimonials or free consultation don't write these words in. Everyone does this. Instead for testimonials you could write, see our 153 happy patients. How much better is that than simply just writing "Testimonials"?!?! As I said before, you want as many qualified people to click on your ads as possible so use this ad extension to reinforce the benefits of the main claim you've already made in the headline and description of your ad. The more people who click the higher chance you have of converting more people into lifetime patients and clients. Now you've in a great position to move onto the callout extension.

Figure 13.7 showing how to set up sitelink extensions.

Callout Extensions

Now callout extensions are the least exciting of all ad extensions simply because you're limited on what you can say. You don't link anyone to a page like you can with sitelinks. However, callout extensions do have value. As you can see below in figure 13.8, you can see the callout extensions in their position on the ad. Now you can see in this example the extension is very weak meaning there isn't much of an incentive for a person to click this ad which is the same as most ads.

So understand, the purpose of a call out extension in the first place is to offer more information and benefits about the service you're offering. However it's not enough to just write features of your service e.g. free consultation, experienced surgeon etc.

Car Accident Attorneys - Douglas & London, P.C.
[Ad] www.douglasandlondon.com/car-accident ▼ +1 877-963-8172
Top New York City Car Accident Attorneys. You Don't Pay Unless We Win. Call Now!
You Only Pay When We Win · Free Consultation · Call 24/7

Figure 13.8 showing a callout extensions on a Google ad.

You've got to go deeper than that to use callout extensions most effectively.

Therefore, see callouts as you offering the most important benefits of your entire service as a whole. It's simply not enough for you to just write basic features and facts about your service. Those features and facts can come on your landing page but not on your ad because the sole goal is to get attention by differentiating your practice and writing basic features and facts doesn't differentiate you. It makes you appear like a commodity. So as you can see in figure 13.9, all you have to do is simply write the biggest benefit which appeals to the problem your prospects want solving. I'd recommend doing at least 2 callout extensions and a maximum of 4 is a great number to stop at. Once you've done this let's move onto the next ad extension.

Figure 13.9 showing you how to set up callout extensions for your Google ads.

Structured Snippets

Structured snippets can be a very confusing one for most businesses. They appear very much like callout extensions as you can see below in figure 13.91. Even when we look at how to set them optimally you'll also see how similar they appear in the set up.

So what's the purpose of structured snippets? The purpose is similar to what a catalogue does. A catalogue shows you many different products all at once as it gives you a variety to choose from. Simply Adwords is trying to give you as much incentive as possible to offer a variety of your service from Adwords because people feel they have a much greater range of choice than just one service. Many of you may be thinking well there doesn't seem to be much point in using structured snippets if the sole goal in the first place is to acquire as many quality calls as possible for one specific service. Well that may be true but remember the more ad extensions you use the higher relevance you can acquire and as a result the higher your ad can display on Google. The higher your ad can display the more chance you have of acquiring more quality customers.

Personal Injury Lawyers | No Win No Fee Claims | slatergordon.co.uk
[Ad] www.slatergordon.co.uk/Injury-Lawyers/Claims ▾
Top Law Firm With Over 85 Years Of Experience. Contact Us Today For Free Advice
Types: Work Accident Claims, Car Accident Claims, Holiday Claims, Industrial Disease Claims

Figure 13.91 showing a structured snippet extension on a Google ad.

The real question is, how do we set structured snippets up? Well as you can see in figure 13.92, you're simply going to click the drop down menu on the right and click "Review Catalogue" after you've clicked structured snippets at the bottom of your campaign page. Once you've done this, you're then able to select 3 different values which in our case is 3 different services or 3 different components of the same service. Personally I'd recommend 3 different components of the same service e.g. for Invisalign you could mention specific technology, quality of braces and speed of results. Much better this way as you keep focus on the one service you're looking for people to enquire about.

Figure 13.92 showing how to set up structured snippets.

Now you've finished this you're ready to move onto the big guns of Google Adwords itself. Seriously, what you've read so far is going to be nothing as to what you're about to read. So let's jump into this right now.

Chapter 14

Only Chapter You Will Ever Need for Keyword Selection

————— ◆ —————

Dam we're finally here. This topic on keywords is in many ways one of the most misunderstood aspects of Adwords entirely and is one of the easiest mistakes to make. The reason I say this is because normally Google gives you some form of help to push you towards what they feel is a good option for you to use. However with keywords Google gives you ZERO insights whatsoever. You'll see in a moment how simple it is to screw keywords up if you don't pay attention to what I'm about to talk about. Seriously, as Google gives you zero help on this it's critical you pay close attention to what I'm about to say about keywords.

What are the Different Types of Keywords?

Keywords in general. Well this is perhaps the foundation of your entire campaign. First it's important you understand match types and how differently the end result of your campaign will be if you choose the wrong match type. Seriously, this is the easiest aspect to Adwords you can screw up and what's worse is you don't even know you've screwed up. You just assume everything is running smoothly until you come back to your campaign a day later to find out you've blown half your budget. Yes, it's that serious to get this right. So as you can see below in figure 14.1, you'll see the keyword box which is the same box you'll use to decide which keywords you want in a specific ad group which we'll talk about in more depth later.

Figure 14.1 shows where to start typing in your keywords.

As you can see, you're just expected to know what type of match type you want to put into Google. There's no direction here whatsoever. How many of you would be tempted to simply type in the keywords you want to bid on…? Almost every single one of you would do exactly that and what makes it worse is this would be completely wrong especially if you're running a local business campaign. YES WRONG! Let's explain why simply typing in your keywords to the keyword box would be wrong for a local business. Well the first thing is there are 4 different match types of keywords you can go after and they are:

1. Broad Match i.e. keyword *personal injury attorney nyc* allows any of these words by themselves i.e. just injury and your ad would show up.

2. Broad Match Modifier i.e. Using a plus sign to modify parts of the keyword would only allow your ad to show up for the

words inbetween the plus signs i.e. *+personal injury +attorney nyc*.

3. Phrase Match I.e. *"personal injury attorney nyc"* would only allow this order of this phrase to show up but not completely exact e.g. best personal injury attorney nyc.

4. Exact Match I.e. keyword *[personal injury attorney nyc]* would only allow your ads to show up for this specific keyword. No variations whatsoever.

So yes that's quite a handful especially considering when you go to type your keywords out there's no instructions at all. Obviously the reason for this is because Google wants you to spend as much money as possible and using broad match keywords as a local business is one of the fastest ways to blow your entire budget. That's how critical it is to understand what match type is best for you.

Let's start with broad match. So as you can see in figure 14.2 how I've simply typed the keyword as it is. No quotation marks, no brackets no nothing. This is the most tempting way to type keywords into the keyword box because you'd think well that's all you need to do. Of course that's wrong. With broad match if your keyword was personal injury attorney nyc lots of different variations of that keyword would cause your ad to show up I.e. *injury lawyer nyc*, *personal lawyer nyc* etc. This is a very bad situation because you want to bid on these keywords separately so you can control your budget much better. Instead what's happening is you've lost a big portion of your control as your ads will show up for keywords you haven't even selected.

Figure 14.2 shows broad match keywords typed into the keyword box.

The big problem with this is as a local business we're focusing on acquiring quality patients and cases and showing up for all these different variations kills our ability to know the type of people searching and clicking on our ads. Now, broad match can be great if you have the budget and want to look for extra variations of keywords to go after but for the most part most local businesses won't need this. It's simply not necessary.

This brings us to our second type of match keyword and that is broad match modifier. Now with broad match modifier you're allowing yourself a little more control because you've selected the parts of the keyword you don't mind variations coming up for e.g. *+personal injury +attorney +nyc* would allow variations of keywords to use the words personal injury, attorney & nyc.

As you can see in figure 14.3, you'll be able to see how you do this for your keywords. Once again, as it's a broad match based keyword strategy it's best to not focus on this for the time being. Now the only exception to this rule is if the keywords you want to go after have very low traffic and you need more traffic to acquire patients and cases through your door. Only in this case should a local business use broad match modifier. As most local businesses won't be in this situation I'd strongly recommend avoiding this match type and focusing on the next 2 variations we'll be talking about. For those of you who are interested, go to this link right here to read more about each individual match type as there's an extra 50 pages which could be written on each match type alone:

> https://support.google.com/adwords/answer/2497836?hl=en-GB

<

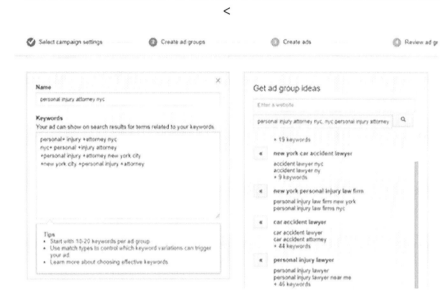

Figure 14.3 shows broad match modifier keywords in the keyword box.

This brings us to phrase match. Phrase match keywords, broad match modifier and exact match keywords are going to be the 3 types a local business must focus on. Now there is some debate as to whether you should use exact match and broad match modifier instead of phrase match but from my experience I'd recommend exact match, broad match modifier and phrase match. It's your call though which strategy you'd like to take. So as you can see in figure 14.4 below, all phrase match keywords must be signalled like so: *"Personal Injury attorney nyc"*. When you put quotation marks around a keyword like that you're signalling to Google it's a phrase match keyword. So now we're moving into a type of keyword where you the business owner have much more control over the type of variation which you allow your ads to show up for.

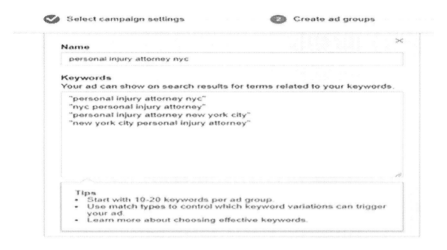

Figure 14.4 showing phrase match keywords in the keyword box.

With phrase match keywords all you're doing is simply having a specific phrase which must come up every time for your ads to show but you can allow other words to be used before or after the phrase, just not in between. For example, you use the keyword *"Women's hats"* so your ad won't show up for *"women's red hats"* but can show up for *"buy women's hats"* or *"women's hats high quality"*. The reason I recommend this match type to use for your campaigns as a local business is because often times the searcher won't type in exactly the keyword you've bid on.

Remember people don't just search rigidly for what they want so you cannot expect people to always type in *"personal injury attorney nyc"* and expect all people to search this way. Some definitely will and those keywords do great. But it doesn't make sense to miss out on all these quality searchers who may search *"best personal injury attorney nyc"* instead. So use phrase match keywords wisely.

The final and perhaps most important match types every local business must use is what's called exact match keyword types. Now as you can see in figure 14.5, each exact match keyword is categorised using [personal injury attorney nyc]. Brackets around the keyword like this indicate to Google this is an exact match type keyword.

So what is the purpose of using an exact match keyword type? Well the purpose is because local businesses for the most part are heavily limited on the amount of traffic they can get because they're in a specific city. Therefore it's key they take advantage of the city specific based keywords as much as possible. Simply using broad match for a keyword such as *plastic surgeon dallas* doesn't yield much into a quality search for a local business. The key is for a local business to be as specific as humanly possible with their keywords.

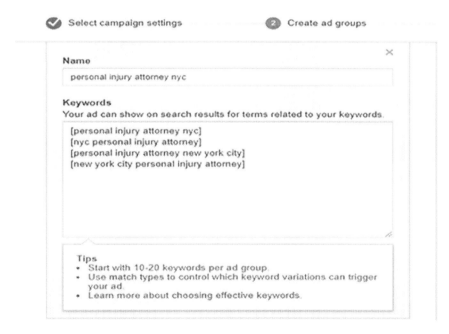

Figure 14.5 showing exact match keywords in the keyword box.

After this many of you might be asking well, what exactly does an exact match keyword do that a phrase match or broad match keyword doesn't do? To that I'd say great question.

Exact match keywords as briefly explained above don't allow any variations of your ad to show up on the keywords you've bid on. A great example would be you bidding on [cosmetic dentist chicago]. Using this keyword type means only this phrase and this phrase in this order will allow your ad to show. If a person typed in cosmetic dentistry chicago then your ad wouldn't show because exact match requires the exact keyword to be typed out into Google for your ad to show. Now some of you may say well this sounds silly because you'd want smaller variations of keywords to allow your ad to show I.e. cosmetic dentist chicago and cosmetic dentistry chicago to both show. That isn't a problem because you'd simply bid on both keywords. You don't need variations to show up for exact match to be highly effective.

What's even better is you focus purely on both exact match and phrase match keywords so you get the best of both worlds. On top of which exact & phrase match keywords are superior for businesses on a lower budget. Most businesses aren't going to spend $10,000 a month right out the gate. You need proof of concept first which only comes from starting off on a smaller budget. You can't see proof of concept starting with broad match keywords so don't make it harder on yourself unnecessarily. You keep purely focused keywords and you allow great variations to trigger your ads also.

How the Pros Leverage Granular Account Organisation

At this point, many of you having seen the keyword box yourself and in the images I've created for you here are wondering how many keywords per ad group? Some of you may even be wondering what an ad group is and that's okay also. Let's quickly explain what an ad group is. So remember you have 3 levels:

1. Campaign I.e. targeting, schedule, budget etc.

2. Ad group I.e. grouping specific types of keywords together.

3. Keywords I.e. the words you want your ads to show up for.

An ad group is simply a group which you want to house a specific type of keyword and it's variations. For example if you're a cosmetic dentist in San Diego you might have an ad group for cosmetic dentist and the keywords are shown below in figure 14.6. You see it's only cosmetic dentist based keywords in here. I'm not using keywords like *dentist san diego* or *dentistry san diego.* Only cosmetic dentist and *dentistry san diego* to keep as much focus per ad group as possible. This way you're able to write ads with much greater relevance which in turn increases your quality score and in turn increases the chances of more people enquiring about your service.

This in turn is called granular account organisation and is highly credited towards Adwords master himself Brad Geddes. You're simply ensuring your ad groups are highly specific. You're not putting invisalign keywords in the dentistry ad group because they're not as relevant to each other. So what this means is when you come to write your ad based off the keywords it's going to be harder to have high relevance because you'd be talking about dentistry and be bidding on Invisalign keywords. By all means bid on Invisalign keywords but don't put them in the same ad group as dentistry keywords. Instead give them their own ad group. This skill and alone is what separates the most successful Google Adwords campaigns. Don't take this advice lightly.

Keywords
Your ad can show on search results for terms related to your keywords.

[san diego cosmetic dentist]
[cosmetic dentist san diego]
[san diego cosmetic dentistry]
[cosmetic dentistry san diego]

Figure 14.6 showing granular organisation based keywords.

As a result you're going to want roughly 8-10 ad groups so you have 2-4 ad groups per keyword type which we spoke about before in a previous chapter I.e. city specific keywords, problem based keywords, symptom based keywords etc. This ensures you have plenty of keywords to play around with to start you off.

On top of which you've exhausted a good amount of options for your ads to show up too so you know you're not going to be heavily limiting your ability to acquire more patients and clients through Google. Once you've done that make sure you don't under use the amount of keywords per ad group. What I mean by this is most people find a few keywords they want to use and just use 2-3 i.e. *personal injury attorney nyc* and *nyc personal injury attorney.*

The problem here is Google will penalise you for not using at least a bare minimum of 5 keywords per ad group. Remember Google wants you to spend as much money on their platform as possible and if you're only using 2 keywords they know you're trying to limit your budget. In return they'll limit the reach of your ads. Not a great situation. No one wants the benefits of their service to reach a severely limited amount of people. The moral? Use at least 4 keywords per ad group.

Long Tail vs Short Tail Keywords

Ah my favourite part next regarding keywords. Long tail vs short tail keywords. Again it's an area a lot of businesses get wrong so it's important we discuss it. So what even are long tail and short tail keywords? Short tail keywords are keywords typically of 3 words or less e.g. *injury lawyer chicago*. Long tail keywords are keywords which are 3 words or longer I.e. *personal injury attorney los angeles*. The combination of both of these keywords is key but it's important you know where to start. It's much more effective for you to start with keywords of 4 words and below because you know these types of keywords have a good amount of searches already.

As you can see in figure 14.7, you can see data of the keyword breast augmentation phoenix and see it's already got 200+ searches a month. You want to start with this length of keyword because you know it's working already.

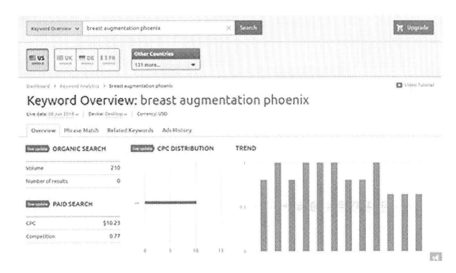

Figure 14.7 showing data of a specific medium tail keyword already performing.

Once you've had success with these types of keywords then you can start to go with 1-2 word keywords and 5+ word keywords. Remember, 55% of all Adwords searches have 3+ words in them. Once you see the success already with one type of keywords then it makes a whole lot more sense to start looking for great variations which are either very short or very long keywords. The point here is to keep finding angles which you can continually use to advertise on. You must not just find the most effective keywords at 3-4 words and stop there. You must keep testing to find bigger and perhaps better keywords you can use your competitors don't likely know about. Why? Because it takes a effort to figure this out. Most businesses & agencies don't want to put in the time.

Misspelled Keywords & Why They're so Important to Adwords Success

For some help on variations of keywords to test, you can always try misspelled keywords. The amount of times people fail to spell keywords correctly is incredibly high because most users in the modern world are on their phones and it can be difficult to type 100% accurately on their phone. It's a smaller keypad to type on and often results in errors.

So if you're bidding on *[personal injury attorney houston]* then it would make sense to test *[personl injury attorny houston]*. It's very easy to make these kind of spelling mistakes which means if you haven't put these variations into your ad groups then you could be missing out on a lot more patients & clients than you thought. Remember, most of your competitors won't do this. So if you have a competitor who spends $30,000 a month on Adwords you can easily steal customers away from them by bidding on the misspelled keywords too. It's interesting how these small little hacks can result in monumental gains :)

Wow this has been a long chapter. But don't worry we're almost at the end of the road. We don't have much longer to go in this chapter. However the final topic of conversation in this chapter has to be negative keywords. Yes you heard me correctly, negative keywords.

Your Failure to Properly Deal with Negative Keywords will Crush Your Campaigns

What are negative keywords? Negative keywords are simply keywords which didn't work for you meaning you had a high CTR but low conversions or you had a low CTR and low to zero conversions. Either way these keywords didn't convert well for you so what would be the point in continuing to keep these keywords in your ad group? Exactly, there isn't much of a point. So if keywords don't work do we just throw them out completely? Not exactly. What we do is put all the keywords which haven't been working for us on the negative keyword list. The reason we do this is because we want to avoid any kind of chance our ad shows up for this variation especially if we're doing phrase match keywords which I recommend every local business do.

As you can see below in figure 14.8, all you have to do to access your negative keyword list is by:

1. Going into your campaign.

2. Clicking on the keywords tab.

3. Clicking on the negative keywords tab and then going from there.

Figure 14.8 showing how to type keywords into your negative keyword list.

Remember this is a very important step. You don't want to be using phrase match, keywords which aren't converting and not put them on your negative keyword list. You also want to make sure you type in all your competitor's names inside your negative keyword list as it's not worth spending the money to show up for these keywords. Also remember if the keyword you used didn't work & was an exact match keyword then make sure you put brackets around it in the negative keyword list. Don't just put broad match in there and it expect it to be okay. The key here is to ensure you're not spending any money whatsoever on keywords which don't work so you can maximise your entire budget into keywords which do convert. It's quite simple really. Once you get the hang of this you'll end up emailing me laughing in joy over how simple using negative keywords is. It sounds daunting at the start but I promise you, it really isn't.

Dam that was quite a long chapter. You're now ready to start selecting the different type of ad you want to run and after this you'll be ready to start writing your ad copy which I would argue is the best part of Adwords as a whole. You get to craft out specific sentences and phrases whilst trying to fit the character count. Okay maybe it's not that fun... Let's dive into it right now.

Chapter 15

Change the Game
with Your Ad Choice

———————◆———————

Well this chapter is destined to be an interesting one. The only downside of Google to Facebook is simply the amount of quality options a local business can successfully use to generate more quality patients and clients. Now despite the fact you're a little limited, this doesn't take away the power of Text ads themselves.

The Importance of Text Ads

We've got 4 main ads which are going to be highly relevant for you as a local business. Now I will say there are more options such as mobile app engagement and shopping ads but for a local business they're not relevant to you right now. We only want to focus on the types of ads which have the highest relevance to your current situation so let's do just that.

Once again, as there's plenty of options to choose from it's very easy to choose an ad type which doesn't benefit you. I mean if you don't know what's good and what's bad then how are you supposed to know what works? So let's start with the ad you're going to use the most and that is the "Text Ad".

As you can see below in figure 15.1, you'll see the actual structure of the text ad. For now let's focus on the importance of the text ad.

Figure 15.1 showing various different lawyers using a text ad.

The text ad is the type of ad you and your competitors will use the most. It's very simple and it's one of the easiest ways to get your message across to the specific people who searched for the most relevant keywords to what you're offering. The 3 biggest benefits of text ads are:

1. It's really easy to qualify specific people you want and don't want as patients.

2. It's really simple for you to maximize your value proposition.

3. It's a helpful ad you can display to people who've searched for the keywords most relevant to your ads.

As I said before, when your ads trigger for the keywords you want to bid on, it becomes much easier to find the highest quality people to advertise in front of. Now some of you may object to the text ad as 99% of your competitors use it. To that I'd say just because your competitors use it doesn't mean you shouldn't. It's still arguably the most helpful ad to acquire the highest quality patients and clients you want to use to grow your business.

Call Only Ads

Call only ads are our next stop. At first glance considering the fact we're advertising on Google Adwords to get the phone call, logic would tell you this is the best type of ad to do exactly that… Right? Well this type of ad has both pros and cons. Just briefly look below at figure 15.2 and you'll see what I mean. Despite the fact it's very easy for prospects to see your number and give you a call, from my experience call only ads don't perform as well as text ads. My theory on this is because:

1. You come across as pitching with the number in the headline.

2. You don't get as much space to convey your value proposition.

Figure 15.2 showing the structure of a text ad.

Now does that mean you shouldn't use call only ads? Far from it. I said they don't perform as well as text ads. I didn't say they don't perform at all. So I'd highly recommend starting with text ads and using call only ads as a direct test with your text ads. If both work great then you've got 2 different ad types which are working successfully for you. If not then you've found an ad type which isn't effective and that's good. You won't waste anymore of your time & money on what doesn't work. The moral? Use call only ads sparingly.

Dynamic search ads. Well these are very interesting especially contrasted against text and call only ads. Your ability to convey your value proposition is the same which is similar to text ads. Yet these ads show up not based on the keywords you've bid on but Google will show your ad based on your landing page being crawled on by Google. Told you this is an interesting ad type! So as you can see in figure 15.3 below here, you can still write out and convey your value proposition. But the biggest downfall with this type of ad is you have less control over when your ad shows up and exactly what your ad shows up for.

You could have a completely unrelated word on your landing page to your offer which makes the point of what you're trying to say but Google sees that and triggers your ad to show up for it. You've now paid money for a completely irrelevant search and if anything will just annoy people in your city because you're not showing ads for relevant keywords. So the advice I recommend is similar for call only ads, use them sparingly.

They're 100% worth a test but only once you've established success with text ads first. Once you've got that initial test sorted then you can start to do more experiments surrounding things like dynamic search ads. It's the same with making a meal. You have fundamental ingredients which work everytime and when you want to get a little crazy and test new ideas you throw them in. You don't start with the crazy ideas. You test them once you've already established success.

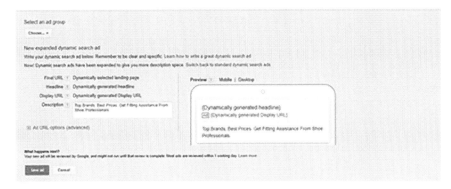

Figure 15.3 showing the structure of a dynamic search ad.

Display Ads

Now we're only going to cover display ads because display advertising is a completely different animal in it's own right. Many of you won't know what the display network is and that's perfectly fine as I'm about to explain it. Don't worry. So as you can see in figure 15.4 that's a display ad I simply picked up off the internet. The main difference between the display network and the search network (the entire framework of this book) is:

1. Display network you can shows ads on millions of different websites all over the internet including a competitor's site. Search network causes your ad to show up when people search in Google itself.

2. Display advertising can reach millions more people simply because you don't have to view them just on the Google search engine.

3. Display ads as you can see in figure 15.4 are based more on pictures similar to Facebook advertising rather than just text unlike text ads.

Figure 15.4 shows an display ad example on YouTube.

Remember the display network is great for scaling out your business but don't focus on it until you're having very strong consistent success with the Google search network.

Finally, that's all the different ads I'd recommend a local business using and trying out. You've got 4 options there but as I said before, start with Text ads and once you've got success there start using the other types of ads. You'll find 90% + of your success on the Google search network will come from text ads so even though they appear a bit boring in the broad scheme of things they're still the most effective for any local business.

So if you enjoyed this chapter then get ready for what's coming. One of the most important chapters in the book and in many ways one of the 2 biggest reasons for my client's astounding success with Adwords as a whole. Of course we're talking about copywriting and we're about to dive into it right now.

Chapter 16

Monkeys Write Better
Ad copy than Most Humans

———◆———

Wow we're finally at this chapter. This skill alone can at least quadruple your current Adwords success if you follow what I recommend. Seriously, this chapter right here is so incredibly powerful you're going to feel so happy whilst reading this. On top of which a lot of the copy theory and strategies for Adwords aren't in other Google Adwords books. This is how powerful and unique this chapter is going to be for your business.

The Fundamentals of World Class Google Adwords Copy

So let's jump into it. One of the reasons people don't particularly like Adwords copy is simply because you can be seen as highly limited due to the amount of characters Google allocates you to write for your ads. Frankly when I first looked at writing copy on Google I was getting so frustrated simply because of how difficult it was for me to convey the information I wanted to convey to the audience of each client.

So as a result because people really struggle with good quality copy on Google it means the people who win at Google are the ones who spend the most money. This is because if you spend the most money you have a higher chance of being ranked #1 in Google for the keywords you go after. But remember the good news is these businesses are highly vulnerable because they're heavily reliant on the amount of money they're spending to be in the top position. They're not relying on copy or clickfraud technology or even skill at the platform to get them there. So for those business owners fed up of having to spend ridiculous amounts of money on Google just to compete with your competitors then you're going to love this chapter even more.

A fantastic way to look at Adwords copy is you aren't limited with the amount of characters you can use in your ads. If you view Adwords copy as limited then it will be limited. A better way of looking at it is massive clarity of the benefits you can provide other businesses can't. Remember anything but clarity kills you here simply because you run out of space. What's even better is because most agencies aren't highly skilled at copywriting for Adwords and in general it means it's much easier for you to overtake your competitors. The harder something is the better because you know the less competition you're going to have. It's far easier to write:

"50 years experience. Call us Today for your Free consultation" than put really effort and thought into distilling down your message you want conveyed in Adwords. So hopefully you won't write copy this way anymore and to give you an example of how bad this copywriting is then pay attention to figure 16.1 below. The main thought which should cross your mind is what's the difference between all of these plastic surgeons…? The answer is I'm sure there's considerable difference between each surgeon because it's likely each surgeon has a particular style of surgery they feel is better than the rest. Yet, why isn't this uniqueness and value communicated? Well one answer I would propose is because most agencies don't ask what a business

owner's specific value is and the second answer is because it takes real effort to distil your uniqueness and value down into only 90 characters in your description.

Figure 16.1 showing a Google page result of plastic surgeons in New York City.

As a result, what you see in figure 16.1 is where your campaigns will be heading unless you pay attention to what I recommend in this chapter. Writing general copy like that gets general patients and clients because there's no specification in the copy shown above of what types of patients each surgeon would like. They instead just state their expertise and the service they offer. What's the result? The result is most searchers will simply go to the ad in position 1 because they don't know any better.

The natural response is go and call up whoever is in position 1 because the assumption is they're the best even though we all know that isn't true. As I said many times before, the best expertise doesn't guarantee victory. The best marketing does. Therefore if you're frustrated at seeing competitors beating you who aren't nearly as good as you at what you offer and don't provide the value you offer then it's time to make a change. It's time to finally start getting a grip on how to separate your business on Adwords for the better.

It's the exact same with my agency. For most of you it's difficult for you to choose who's the best agency to work with because all agencies seem to offer Google Adwords, Facebook Advertising, SEO etc. How are you supposed to know who's the best? Well you don't know until you've wasted money. This was exactly the reason I changed the focus of my agency to:

Differentiating business owners from their Competitors through their unique value to acquire more quality patients without excessive spending.

As a result far more people were happy to work with me because they knew exactly what I did and how I was different from everyone else. This should be the same with your practice. People should instantly know the exact value you offer your competitors don't or at least don't communicate. So now, it's time to talk about constructing a USP.

The Easiest way to Construct a Unique Selling Proposition

The USP. What is a USP? Well for those who don't know a USP stands for Unique Selling Proposition/Point and is simply the message and value you offer your competitors either can't or don't offer. Why are we even talking about this? Because it's a waste of time to jump into any advertising if you don't know how to differentiate your business in the first place. If you don't differentiate yourself you then appear like everyone else which makes acquiring new quality patients very difficult unless you're very famous in your particular city.

So how do you go about creating a USP? Well for most of you, you already know the value you can offer to patients. You're just not communicating it yet! You have to start at knowing the value your competitors offer in their service including how much they charge, success of their service etc. Once you've done this, start to analyse your service and your personal skill at the service you're offering.

Now you've got both pieces of information here you can start to craft out a quality USP e.g. Acquire X benefit without having to lose X. The reason this structure of a USP is so important for Adwords is not only the length to fit into the characters you have to play with but also the psychology behind it.

You don't have a huge amount of characters to work with in the first place which means your message & USP have to be EXTREMELY clear. On top of which when people don't have a specific desire and they see someone trying to help them acquire it they start to worry about what they'll lose in the process.

Humans know that often times in order to gain something they have to give something up and it's the giving up part which most people don't like because they hate losing anything. No human likes to lose something. As a result you're framing your service on Google to give them X & X enormous benefits whilst at the same time not losing X & X. This is the main copy strategy behind Adwords so let's go deeper into this to give you an even greater understanding.

Every one of your prospects has multiple desires. Everyone knows that. However the biggest problem you'll see especially in figure 16.1 as you've already seen is most copy isn't written to your prospect's desires. It's instead all about them copy meaning all about the business and service instead of being copy all about the prospect and what the prospect can get out of working with you. Understand, the prospect doesn't care about anything else but finding the solution to their specific problem and if you're not writing to their desires then what reason does a person have to work with you?

Beverly Hills Cosmetic Dentist - Arthur Glosman DDS
Ad www.arthurglosmandds.com/ ▾
Beverly Hills Top 5 Star Dentist. Check out our before & after smiles here! Permanent Solution

Figure 16.1 showing all about the business copy instead of all about the prospect and the prospect's desires.

So within every single person there is the desire to gain something and a desire to not lose something. From my experience each person on average has at least 4 different desires:

1. Tangible desire to gain I.e. More money.

2. Intangible desire to gain I.e. More confidence.

3. Tangible desire to not lose I.e. Not lose money.

4. Intangible desire to not lose I.e. Don't want to lose pride and confidence.

Yes it's likely you've not gone this deep before and don't worry we'll go into how to frame this best for Adwords. It's still important you're 100% clear on the psychology behind each and every quality prospect who has the potential to work with you. So some of you may be wondering why is there both intangible and tangible desires? Great question.

Tangible desires are surface level desires which people explain as what they want out of the service. The most obvious tangible desire people talk about is a cheap price but don't be fooled by this. On the other hand in reality people are ruled by their intangible desires I.e. want more confidence and don't want to lose any social proof they may already have. This is what they really want but they can't come out and say this is what they want because a person appears stupid. Instead they explain tangible desires which are only really used to justify their intangible desire being met.

Remember, 90% of decisions are made unconsciously and decisions of wanting are made extremely quickly. You don't have to think. You don't have to think about liking chocolate or that girl because you just know. We know what we want. However with spinach you have to convince yourself it's healthy and you want it. We're in the chocolate business. The service you offer must be wanted by your prospect almost immediately.

Once this has been achieved through your copy which we'll go through more in a moment all other outside factors and features such as price, speed of treatment etc become good rationalisers for people to use to purchase. Remember people don't like to lose anything and spending money without any justification results in pain mentally and socially. Therefore features are never reasons to buy. They're justifiers to get the deal done. Seriously, one small piece of copy on your Google ad can make a person crave what you have to offer before they know a whole lot about it. That's how quickly decisions are made because making decisions takes a lot of brain power and if the mind were to consciously make every decision it would be exhausted.

Now let's talk about framing all of this to your ad first, then we'll get to your landing page later. As you can see below:

Benefit, Benefit without having to lose X.

This is the simple formula. As I said before it works very well because it's very clear from the start what you're going to offer & exactly what the person gets for themselves which is what they care about anyway. They only care about how they can benefit and that's it. On top of which you don't just want to throw in ordinary benefits. You want to find out the top solution current customers of yours wanted when they came to work with you in the first place. For example one of the biggest fears of people who undergo Invisalign treatment is they think Invisalign is like braces and of course people don't particularly like braces on their teeth. So an example for a cosmetic dentist could be:

"You can have quality straight teeth for life without painful braces. Call Today!"

Again it's very clear what I'm offering. No thought is required to figure out the offer I'm making here. Now some of you may be thinking well you haven't mentioned a free consultation or what the person gets when they come in for treatment. That's a good point to make.

Remember just because I didn't write consultation or free consultation in the description doesn't mean it's not going to be on our ad. We can put it as a sitelink and/or as a callout extension. People will know the type of consultation they get but the information itself isn't as important as a benefit and what the prospect won't lose. It's important yes for a person to know this but not as important as talking about desires because all your competitors are using "Free Consultation" which means you don't stand out nearly as much.

Even more importantly we're creating an irresistible offer where a person simply can't say no to your offer. Dominos did this best with the infamous USP:

"A fresh hot pizza in 30 minutes or it's free".

It's difficult for a person to say no to a potentially free pizza and it's the same with your offer. Now the whole offer itself will be written in more detail on your landing page but understand this formula I've explained to you works well because it takes enough out of your main offer to build a huge amount of self interest and curiosity. Self interest is one of the greater motivators known to man as every single person only really cares about their own self interest when it comes to finding solutions to their problems.

However, there's something even greater going on here. Look at Domino's USP again just above. What else can you see? Well it's not just the fact you get a pizza quickly but also the fact if you don't get it quickly then it's free. As a result the contrast between gaining and losing here is so high that it makes the offer so difficult to refuse.

Remember people are scanning the environment for contrast between things all the time because it keeps them alive. It's very easy to know the difference between a good person and a bad person when they're talking right next to each other. Without contrast you wouldn't know how good or bad something was. This goes the same with your offer. On Google as I showed in earlier chapters, there isn't really any contrast between all those businesses to make a decision to call one of them. They all appear the same because they all appear to be offering the same thing. As a result how is a person quickly and easily meant to make a decision? Well they can't.

This is the reason we're not just following the formula I gave you but we're increasing the contrast between what the person gains and what the person doesn't lose. The bigger you can make this gap the more irresistible your offer becomes. Seriously empires are built off offers like these so don't take this information lightly because you could expand out your business with a brand new spanking offer. Most of you won't need to change anything to your current service except the way it's been framed on each advertising platform. Now let's discuss fitting this formula into your entire Ad on Adwords right now.

As you can see below in figure 16.2 the entire structure of a potential text ad:

Figure 16.2 shows the structure of a text ad inside Google Adwords.

For your final URL at the top, you can customise this URL to be whatever you like so if you're offering Invisalign then ensure your URL ends with something like world class Invisalign or something like that. Don't overdo this. As long as your URL has part of your main keyword in you're fine. So let's talk about both headline 1 & headline 2 in your text ad. So with regards to each headline you don't have a huge amount of characters to work with and much less than your description box at the bottom. As a result you have to be relevant whilst at the same time displaying benefits. So if you're an divorce attorney and bidding on a keyword like divorce lawyer San Francisco, your structure would be:

Headline 1: Divorce Lawyer San Francisco

Headline 2: Don't Lose Your Case. Call Now

In headline 1 all I've done is repeated the keyword back because it's important we're extremely relevant and following Google's terms and conditions. Some of you may be thinking well you're likely going to have 5+ keywords in your ad group and the initial headline isn't going to be exactly the same as what you write in the box. Don't worry. If your ad groups are highly relevant like I showed you how to do then you're going to be doing great.

On top of which, the first headline indicates the prospect is in the right place which is what would cause them to notice you. If they typed in the divorce attorney based keyword and something else came up, then they wouldn't click on your ad because it's not relevant to what they want. Relevancy is the basis of every single successful ad campaign. However relevancy without good copy won't win either because you may get attention by showing your relevant but you won't keep attention without good copy.

Headline 2 is arguably the hardest part of every single ad. You only have 30 characters which means virtually every single formula people suggest out there won't work. Instead simply point out something they don't want to lose and an immediate call to action. This will lead the prospect to do one of 2 things. Either call you right away or then read your description.

Remember you can't just expect a person to read your description if your headlines are poor. This is one of the greatest misperceptions of online advertising which is if you write a whole ad even a very small one like Google then people will read the whole thing. Sorry to disappoint you on that one but they won't. Unless your ad starts off interesting then there's no way they're going to read your whole ad and why they should they? You've given the person no real incentive to keep reading. This is the reason our second headline hits on a key benefit of what they don't want to lose and curiosity to find out more which is key. The finding out more part is very important to Google and advertising in general.

Interestingly enough the display URL is surprisingly read a lot too which you wouldn't initially expect considering it's not the most glamorous looking piece of copy in the world to read. However it's still important. Personally at this stage, I like:

First box: Get X benefit I.e. Win your Case

Second box: Consultation/free consultation.

Once again you're telling the person a specific benefit they can acquire and the means with which they can acquire it. Remember a free consultation or a paid consultation isn't important because it's free or it doesn't cost very much money. It's important because you're explaining to the other person the means of how they can cash in on the benefits you're promising. That's the key. If you didn't mention some kind of consultation then you'd leave the prospect confused of how they'd get these benefits in the first place.

The consultation simply adds to the clarity of where the prospect has to go. Without it you'd be struggling to get action out of people. It's easy to think you can skip some of this stuff but I've skipped everything out you don't already need anyway. I've done the heavy lifting for you so you only have to implement what I'm recommending.

Now we're moving onto the final aspect of your ad which is your description. We've heavily spoken about the original formula above and that is largely going to be used in the description of your ad you can see below. Once more, the description is where you have the greatest leverage to write enough of your irresistible offer to get people to your landing page or call you.

Remember we're not getting people to buy right off our ad but instead inducing one of 2 actions. Either, people will call you right up from the call extension or they'll click through on your ad to your landing page you've got set up. We're simply selling the next step of the sales process. We're not selling the service right away but instead selling the necessary next step to get them to want to pay for your service. It's the exact same as a date with a man or a woman. You wouldn't ask them to marry you right on the first date or at least I hope you wouldn't. You'd ask them for either their number or social media first or potentially ask them to a coffee. Then you'd progress nicely from there.

As for this example keyword, a description you could write is:

"Win your case & keep your house without losing your children. Call Today!"

Very simple. One of the biggest fears of a lot of men and women especially men is they'll lose their house in a divorce battle and one of the strengths of the attorney we're using here is winning back large assets such as the house.

On top of which, you can see this ad doesn't appeal to everyone. Younger couples without children won't respond to this ad because we've specified we only want cases of men and women who have children and often this is because these families can pay the divorce attorney much more to win their case. So it's the best of both world's here. On top of which it's important we briefly discuss the importance of qualification.

Qualification is simply a word to describe specifying the type of case or patient you're looking to work with. Most business don't to work with every type of case or patient not because they're mean but because their personal expertise doesn't reach to every single person.

Therefore if you don't qualify for the type of person you're looking to work with then how do you expect these types of people to know they're the right person for you? As a result you leave yourself completely helpless to the type of person ringing up because you've not said exactly who you want to work with. This is one of the reasons many of you get lots of calls from people asking for a price comparison or a feature comparison because they see you as general so of course they want the cheapest price.

Remember specialists only work with specific types of people and what makes a person a specialist is because they're an expert at solving a few specific problems other people in their city can't solve. You can't be an expert at everything so when people can see from your ad you're the authority at solving a specific problem and helping a specific type of person, then you're going to reduce those "price callers" by upwards of 90%. Yes 90%! Crazy right? Now we've got your entire Google Adwords copy sorted, let's move onto landing page copy and website copy for maximum effectiveness.

How Do I Write Quality Copy for My Landing Page?

Oh landing pages. How these are often times so screwed up by most agencies you work with. Now for those of you who are having great success from Adwords, you may say we're doing great and acquiring lots more cases and patients than we used to. To that I'd say, that may be true but what you may not be aware of is how much business you're losing from using average landing pages. Now I'm not saying every landing page is average. I'm saying most of them are including the top businesses doing millions a year in revenue which is even scarier. It leaves them extremely open to losing their top position on Adwords because they're not out performing their competition but instead out spending. Out spending your competition isn't a healthy long term strategy to win. So let's take a look at figure 16.2 right below here.

Figure 16.2 showing a 5/10 landing page.

What do you see right away which is wrong from this landing page? I don't see one specific problem they solve no other attorney can solve. Attorneys out of all businesses struggle the most with grasping this concept. They think well we all offer personal injury representation so how am I supposed to differentiate myself? Well yes as I've said before you all fundamentally offer the same service but it's the specific benefits and value you as an attorney can offer other attorneys can't e.g. win cases much faster, more aggressive so perhaps that increases your win percentage.

Obviously I don't know your business as well as you do but the point stands you must communicate specific value you can offer other attorneys can't. Otherwise you end up with a landing page like figure 16.2 above. It's not inherently average because of the design but because it's no different to other landing pages. It's simply, if you've been in any kind of accident or personal injury then we're the firm for you. But why are you the business for me? *You've not specified one problem you can solve or one piece of value you can offer me other businesses can't give me.*

On top of which there's lots of information on this page which isn't particularly helpful either. Remember information is helpful but it's specific types of information I.e. desires the person gets when working with you, benefits they get etc that is important information. Plus it's the information which is the most important to the prospect. Remember, it's very easy to overload people with lots of information. We think, well they want information so let's just give them lots of it to help them make a decision. But it doesn't help them make a decision.

As we said earlier, most information only helps a person rationalise the decision they've already made to either work with you or not. So DON'T OVERLOAD YOUR LANDING PAGES WITH LOTS OF INFORMATION.

Understand the human mind can only take so much information and if it's complicated it takes a lot of brain power to figure out what you're saying and this annoys the heck out of people. So to start fixing your landing pages you're going to want to do the following:

1. One bold headline solving a specific problem your competitors can't solve e.g. Introducing your opportunity to acquire X, X & X benefit without losing X, X & X desire.

2. Bullet point the benefits your service has to offer right after. Yes bullet points.

3. Number out the steps the person has to take to get their consultation I.e. call you, book appointment with receptionist, come in for consultation etc.

4. If you're very well known in your city you can talk a bit about your experience below this. (This is the least important).

Remember, the most important factor in your landing pages is not only what problem and value you offer but also can you even solve the person's problem in the first place. They want to know how you can help them better than your competitors can because once they know this information it becomes nice and easy to make the decision to work with you. Now, we've simply expanded on our initial description we wrote in our ad which isn't just going to help your relevance with Google but will also help prospect's ability to know they're in the right place. The last thing a prospect wants to do is click an ad and end up in the wrong place.

Now some of you may be wondering why we've used bullet points to list out the most important benefits to each prospect rather than just write a paragraph.

Understand it takes a lot of mental effort for a person to read a paragraph and mental effort to the brain is a threat because it takes a lot of mental energy to read. *The brain likes to conserve as much energy as possible because your brain wants to keep you alive.* Instead you want to focus on giving each prospect eye relief which is a term invented by the late Gary Halbert to suggest the last thing you want to do is send people to a page where it looks daunting to read.

You have to make it so simple to start reading because once a person starts reading the job becomes easier to get them to convert. But if they don't even start reading in the first place then you've got ZERO chance of converting them to a lifetime patient or client.

This is one of the reasons when people visit your website to check you out they leave very quickly because you've not said what problem or value you can solve & provide your competitors can't. Plus you have a lot of text jumbled together which provides very little eye relief.

On top of which it's important to remember prospects aren't coming to your page or ad completely fresh. They're already into their day and as a result are either slightly fatigued or heavily fatigued so there can be no room for error here. Little mistakes like jumbling your text together can easily cost you $30,000 in lost patients in a month and in many cases over $200,000 a month in lost revenue because of the people who had no tolerance to read your content.

Now the final aspect to understand on landing pages here is the reason we've numbered the steps for the prospect to take to get their problem solved. People are terrified by the uncertainty and they like to know upfront what is required for them to get the specific result they're looking for.

Now most of you have done this but have done it in a paragraph form which makes it difficult to read and provides little eye relief. We use numbers because it makes it very simple for any person to follow what needs to be done. On top of which it's very easy for people mentally to see themselves doing the actions itself to come in for an appointment. If a person can't imagine themselves doing something then chances are they won't do it because it's not within their reality. So writing out steps 1 by 1 will dramatically increase the amount of people who give you a call because they know exactly what to expect and exactly what needs to be done.

Create a Common Enemy in Your Marketing

The final thing we're going to talk about here before we end this chapter is creating a common enemy. People in general love to blame other people and never like to blame themselves and as a result it's extremely simple to form a bond with a person who you've never met simply by disliking or even hating a specific person or an organisation. Take Donald Trump & Hilary Clinton. If you hate either of those people and you find a person who hates them too you've instantly formed a connection with them without having really done anything.

So how do we apply this to Google Adwords? Well one thing you can test with is by finding the common enemy in your market so for personal injury attorneys the common enemy could be the big bad companies who don't want to give you compensation. For plastic surgeons the common enemy could be the people in a person's life who constantly ridicule them for not looking a certain way. The point is you find an immediate source of common ground to build trust so I'll give you a great example for a personal injury attorney:

Want to let the big bad companies take your money? We can help. Call Us!

Now I know I gave you a formula earlier for Adwords which works better than any formula I've found because it separates you right from the start. It tells the person what they can and precisely what they don't lose. But remember the good news is you want to test different factors and try other angles. You might find this approach works better for your actual copy. That doesn't mean you don't create a proper USP and a fantastic offer. It just means the copy on your ad on Google you use might be slightly different. We'll go into testing in more depth later but understand for now the importance of finding common ground with new prospects and testing different angles to your marketing.

Phew that was a long chapter. Next we're going to dive face first into a principle which brings your copy together. This one principle if done improperly can severely reduce the impact your copy and USP has on your city. It's that important.

Chapter 17

Quality Score Will Take You Beyond the Moon

———— ◆ ————

Well this chapter is going to blow your mind of how important it is to get this right. If you don't get this right then regardless of how good your copy is you're not going to do nearly as well as you could had you got this right. What I've shown you in terms of copy and clickfraud technology will dramatically improve your campaigns beyond imaginable. Yet it's still important you sort your quality score out.

How Important is Quality Score to Your Google Adwords Success?

So what is quality score? Well as you can see below in figure 17.1, quality score is a part of a process Google uses called Ad rank which determines how high your ads will rank against your competitors. So obviously the higher the ad rank the higher your ads are going to show on the search engine. It's that simple. Now ad rank as you can see below in figure 17.1 is composed of:

1. How much you're spending per click.

2. How high your quality score is.

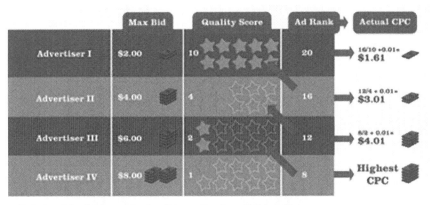

Notice how Advertiser I can pay less for a higher position due to his high quality score.

Figure 17.1 showing ad rank.

Now as you can see below this time in figure 17.2 what quality score is actually composed of. Quality score is composed of:

1. How relevant your ad copy is to your search result.

2. How high your Click through Rate is.

3. How relevant your landing page is to your ad and keyword you're bidding on.

Figure 17.2 showing components of quality score.

How Does Quality Score Affect Your Ad Rank?

Before I explain each of these factors first understand, if your quality score is a 6 or less then you cannot expect to rank consistently in position 1 because you're not following Google's rules well enough. Plain and simple. So despite every new piece of information I've shared with you so far in this book, the information's effectiveness will be limited unless your ads are ranking in position 1 which is one of the key goals you're looking for when advertising on Google in the first place. We're advertising to outrank your competitors whilst spending 3-7 times less than them. We don't want to spend 3-7 times less than them & still let them take a lot of business from you when you may deserve it more.

What makes it worse is your competitors who don't differentiate themselves whatsoever as proven already and don't particularly have great copy will keep outranking you unless your quality score is 8+. Mostly your competitors are outranking you based on the amount of money they're spending which as I've said before isn't a good strategy because you're left extremely vulnerable to being outranked and losing your top position on Google. No one wants to lose their top position.

Fastest ways to Increase Your Quality Score

So now you understand the importance of quality score and getting it right, let's dive into how to actually increase your quality score.

Remember, you can't have an 7+ quality score, spend a very low amount of money and outrank your top competitors if they're spending 10 times more than what you plan to spend. You still have to be willing to spend money on Google but it doesn't have to be nearly as much as what your competitors are spending. Remember that.

Let's start with relevance of your copy to the keyword you're bidding on. So as you can see below in figure 17.3 a picture of a test ad against the keyword I would be bidding on. The reason the keyword is the first words I write in the headline is because I want to ensure Google see I'm trying to bid on keywords I have the most relevance to. I'm not trying to bid on keywords where I can get easy customers and patients if I don't have strong relevance.

San Diego Cosmetic Dentist - Not Sure Who to Trust?

Figure 17.3 showing myself using relevance in my 1st headline to the keyword I'm bidding on.

Think about it this way. If you type something into Google which is very specific for example "Blepharoplasty Columbus". You typed this in because you're looking for a surgeon who does this specific service in this specific city. So how would you feel if other treatments started coming up in the same city and other cities?

I bet you wouldn't feel super happy because you typed something into Google looking for a very specific search result and instead you got other listings which aren't nearly as relevant to what you wanted in the first place. This is what you must avoid. You never bid on keywords which you don't have complete relevancy to and you don't write copy which isn't relevant to the keyword either. If you don't have a relevant ad then of course Google is naturally going to show your ad much lower in the search results because Google's priority is ensuring their searchers are happy and they're not going to be happy if irrelevant listings are showing up.

How high is your click through rate? So as we've already discussed earlier, click through rate is the amount of impressions I.e. the amount of people who've seen your ad divided by the amount of people who click your ad. For example, 1000 people see your ad and 3 people click it so you have a 3% click through rate. Simple right? But how is click through rate important to Google? Well in Google's world the ads which get clicked on the most are the ones which make them the most money. The ads which don't get clicked on nearly as much aren't going to get the amount of attention compared to other ads as they're going to make Google less money.

Okay, well how do you get a higher click through rate? Well as we've discussed before the easiest and fastest way is to 1. Bid on keywords where your offer is highly relevant and 2. improve your ad copy.

As I've said before ad copy truly does make the difference in every single form of advertising you do. It's difficult to comprehend in the beginning that more people will buy what you offer because of the different words on the page but once you understand this you'll be relentless about improving your copy. It's the number 1 skill which can bring your business more quality patients and clients. Therefore go back to the previous chapter where we go much more in depth on copy so you'll be able to write extremely effective ads. Either way the important thing to note here is better ad copy will result in more people clicking and responding to your ad compared to bad ad copy. This rule stands the test of time every single time you advertise.

Landing pages. Oh how these are messed up for quality score. The annoying part with landing pages is they're the biggest pain out of all 3 factors to go back and change simply because it takes more work and thought. But I can tell you a good landing page is going to be one of your greatest assets in acquiring more quality patients and cases to your practice. So as you can see below in figure 17.4 what a bad landing page looks like in terms of quality score. I'm not commenting on whether the page converts I'm commenting on whether the page violates Google's terms or not. As you can see, there isn't the keyword placed within the headline of the offer and the keyword was "Plastic Surgeon NYC". It's critical you simply carry on the headline you wrote in your ad in the description box to ensure:

1. Your landing page is relevant to your ad copy.

2. Your landing page is relevant to the keyword you're bidding on.

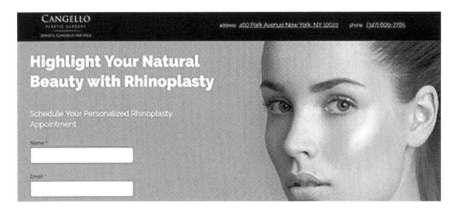

Figure 17.4 showing a poor landing page in the eyes of Google terms of service.

It's not enough to have an offer and stick it on a landing page. It's not enough at all. You've got to do better than that otherwise your ads are going to rank much lower than they should be. Remember you always want your ads to be in position 1, never lower than that so you must do everything in your power to ensure Google wants to rank you higher. When you have Google more on your side than on your competitors, you'll start to win almost everytime.

Once you've put your keyword in your headline on your landing page and continued your description from your ad into your landing page you're good to go. You'll also be able to see your quality score in your account as you can see in figure 17.5 below. You'll see how well you're doing in the 3 areas of quality score so you know what to improve each time.

Figure 17.5 showing how you can view your quality score.

Now let's move onto creating fantastic landing pages your competitors can only sit in awe at. You'll see plenty of examples of bad landing pages in the next chapter so you'll know exactly what to do to ensure you create landing pages Google love to promote. Let's jump into it now!

Chapter 18

Create a Beautiful Island
for your Visitors to Land On

———————— ◆ ————————

Well this one is going to be monumentally important to get right. The reason I make such a bold statement at the start is because not using clickfraud technology and using bad copy is much easier to fix.

On top of which they're much easier to know you've done something wrong and if you know what you've done wrong then you do what you can to correct it. However with landing pages it's difficult to know what's wrong and what isn't working unless you have comprehensive software such as heat map software on there to know where your visitors are focusing on. Either way for most local businesses and agencies, landing pages are the area which don't get the right amount of love. They certainly get lots of love through design but certainly not so in the structure, the conversion rate optimization aspect of the page and the copy itself on the page. Pay close attention because fixing your landing pages could be the final part of the puzzle to making Adwords extremely successful for your practice.

What's the Most Effective Way to Structure My Landing Pages?

Let's start with structure. Okay so as you can see in figure 18.1 a landing page for a plastic surgeon in Dallas I just searched for. Initially looking at the page what do you think is wrong about it? Well for starters there's no headline. Just quickly, for those who are going to complain and say I'm just going to criticize other landing pages and not provide any excellent ones are wrong. I'll directly contrast a great one right after this.

Anyway back to the landing page. There's no headline which means right away the person visiting this page doesn't specifically know what they're going to get from the offer. They have to guess and when you leave a prospect to guess you've lost control of what you want them to imagine about how good your service is. Not having a headline isn't even rare. Most landing pages from local businesses especially attorneys and surgeons don't have a headline because they think they can get away with just outspending their competitors. This works in the short term but you don't get nearly as many quality patients and clients you should going this route in the long term because someone can always come in and spend more than you. It's just like dating a girl because you have money. You can easily lose that girl because someone always can swoop in who has more money than you. For now I'll explain what's wrong with the page and contrast a good page right next to it to demonstrate how you can improve a bad one.

There's simply too much information right at the beginning of the page. Information is important and I'm certainly not saying you shouldn't provide quality factual information on your landing pages. What I'm saying is keep information limited above the fold meaning the first half of the landing page to ensure you maximise your chance of getting the person to call up. As I said before the goal of running Google Adwords is to acquire as many quality phone calls as possible which lead to booked appointments which then turn into lifetime patients and clients who provide handfuls of referrals. You simply don't need to provide this much information at the very start because you're simply going to overwhelm the prospect and cause them to "think about it". There's nothing wrong with thoroughly going through a decision but we all know when a person needs to think about something it just means they're going to delay their decision because they don't want to put in the thought process required to read what you have to say.

As brutal as that sounds, it's the truth. We humans have a very difficult time in breaking down large pieces of information. We like simple information which is very easy to not only read grammatically but also easy on the eyes i.e. not jumbled together as you can see in the below example.

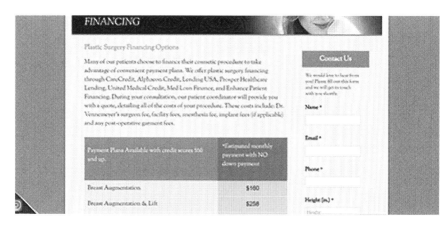

What makes this worse is this is one of the top advertisers in Dallas for plastic surgery and it's getting enquiries. Imagine if you were in this market and applied everything I've told you so far. How much better would your ads do and how many more quality patients would you acquire against them? My guess is you'd do substantially better and acquire far more quality patients.

So the final thing about this page as you can see above is the prices have been listed and too many options have been given to fill out on the form. Understand this, it's not wise to put your prices on your landing page because people are simply going to compare you against your competitors to find the cheapest price. On top of which you've given them enough information to lose curiosity with you and actually come in for an appointment. As a result you've lost the chance to give them their consultation because they've armed themselves with enough information to go out there and find the cheapest price. If you're the cheapest in your city then great but I have the feeling most of you aren't the cheapest. You charge a very fair price for a highly exclusive service and the last thing you want is for potential patients and clients to start comparing your service to your competitors.

What makes this page even worse is there are simply too many options to fill out in the sign up form on the right hand side of the page. The problem here is you've given the prospect too many boxes to fill out which means many people are going to lose focus, get distracted and leave the page and not return. Remember, there is always something tugging at your prospect's attention and if your offer requires a lot of brain power to figure out then they're simply going to zone you out and leave your page. So instead have 3 options:

1. Name

2. Phone Number

3. Email

That's it. Don't overdo it. Let's now directly contrast this with a great landing page.

Now despite the fact I really don't like the fact they've said the price which they're doing because they're the cheapest for Invisalign in London, the rest of the page is much better than the first one I showed you. As you can see in figure 18.2, right away you can see how clear and simple the box is to fill out. It's easy to see and there's much fewer options to fill out as I initially recommended. I don't agree with the message box but either way this is a much bigger improvement than the first.

Figure 18.2 showing a high quality landing page.

What makes this page even better than the first is above the fold of the landing page, you have 3 key benefits listed out like bullet points. As a result it's very easy for a person who visits this landing page to see what they actually get. The benefits are just like any other dentist would offer but these benefits listed here are so much easier to see and read unlike the first page. The first landing page in figure 18.1 didn't really have any bullet points at all. Instead it had lots of text jumbled which was very difficult to read unless you properly sat down and went through it. Let's go even deeper into this page.

The next thing you can spot on the same page in figure 18.3 just below is the use of more images. Images are fantastic and in many ways better than words because you can explain your point in one picture. However with words it could take you a line or two to explain your point. Now I'm not saying words aren't effective but what I'm saying is you must know the various different tools you have at your disposal which you can implement right away. The pictures on this landing page signify the treatment is a successful treatment and plain and simply works. The ideal prospect may be looking for a much better smile to ensure they have a lot more confidence and clearly this picture has some significance to communicating that benefit. So make sure you use both images and words.

Figure 18.3 shows pictures on the same quality landing page as figure 18.2.

Now so far what I've said about this landing page may seem very simple but simple doesn't mean ineffective. Often times the recommendations on landing pages I give people often result in people saying "I already knew that" and to that I'd say, it doesn't matter what you know it matters what you do. Implementation is the key.

On top of which you can see in figure 18.4 the use of video testimonials on this landing page. Now testimonials are extremely important for any advertising regardless of how well known you are. People still like to have a strong level of reassurance other people have been very happy and successful with the treatment the prospect is considering. Understand people like safety and safety almost always is in the number of people who've had success previously with the specific service you're advertising. Video testimonials here are great but could be improved by:

1. Having at least 3 video testimonials for the specific treatment you're offering.

2. Have different types of testimonials I.e. written testimonials with the person's face and name.

Figure 18.4 showing video testimonials on a landing page.

It all adds up and the more proof you have the better position of trust and authority you'll be in. This is a very important position to be in. A key tip on testimonials is you could probably triple the amount of testimonials you're currently using. Seriously they make that much of a difference whether or not to call you.

Now as I've said before, some people won't need a testimonial to call you. They'll like your offer, feel you've connected with their core problems and trust you can solve their problem and as a result give you a call. Remember people trust people who completely understand and convey their current position which is the reason I told you copy is so important and understanding your potential patients and clients on a much deeper level.

As we finish off this sub chapter here, take a look at figure 18.5. You can see how much easier the text is to read. It's only 2 lines long and not jumbled together like the first landing page. The only thing I'd suggest is not allowing the text to go out so wide like that so it comes more to the middle. Once this is done you're moving in the right direction of how you want the text to look on your landing page.

Figure 18.5 showing well separated text on a landing page.

Let's now talk about the structure of a good quality landing page. You now know what you don't want to do on a landing page and you now have some quality information to implement. But what's more important is how to structure this information in the right order on the page itself. So let's outline the exact components you want on every single landing page you create or have created for you:

1. Big bold headline with promise to meet prospect's tangible and intangible benefits.

2. Sub headline to reiterate what the person doesn't have to lose in order to acquire the benefits and Call to action.

3. Direct picture contrast of before and after treatment you're advertising.

4. Factual information on your service in bullet point form to reiterate the benefits of the service.

5. Video testimonials and full testimonial section with at least 3 different testimonials from different people.

6. Reiterate benefits once more with a big call to action.

Okay so this may seem overwhelming at first but don't worry. I promise you once you go through this a few times it will all start to make sense. You have to start somewhere so stick with this and you'll be able to build high quality landing pages or at least understand landing pages with great confidence to outsource to someone else.

Now as I said before, a big strong headline is key and it tells the prospect right away the reason they should be reading your landing page. You can't expect a prospect to give you a call without giving them a strong reason to actually stay on the page. That's simply not fair to expect a person to stay on your landing page without a good reason to so therefore you must communicate the benefits as much as you can upfront. Trust me if there's one thing which will transform your landing pages and as a result increase the amount of quality patients you get from Adwords it's going to be the headline. Here's an example:

Still Looking for a Beautiful Smile? Get Your Free Limited Time Invisalign Consultation Today!

So what have I done here? I've established value and curiosity right away by mentioning it's for a limited time only. I've also made sure once again to acknowledge the initial problem we solve so it's crystal clear if the person doesn't want what you offer they won't ring your office. The last thing you want is people who only seem bothered about the price calling up. This is very important people know this information so they don't end up scheduling a consult only for to find out later they wanted the consult for someone who you don't specialise in treating. I've also narrowed in on the specific biggest pain point which is not having a beautiful smile. The reason this headline works is because it's very easy for the person to see what's in it for them.

They don't have to think about what they can get from you because I've told them right upfront very clearly. This headline alone completely changed my client's way of running their practices' because it focuses in on the value my client can provide other competitors can't. It's a win win for everyone.

As for your sub headline, you want to assume the headline has done a very good job in persuading people to want to give you a call from your landing page because of the marvellous benefits you've displayed. Here's an example:

161

Call Us Now for Your Free Consultation
($297 Value) by Calling (555) 555-5555!

Why does this work? Big heavy call to action telling people very specifically how they can get your offering. I'm quite literally spelling out what they need to do in order to get the free consultation. Therefore I've made it very clear what every potential customer has to do in order to get their consultation.

One other thing I've been testing lately is by explaining what happens after a person calls the number I.e. They'll speak to X receptionist, book their appointment and come in and speak with person X about X. It's been working really well so I'd recommend you give this one a try too.

Very very simple stuff but often overlooked by many businesses and agencies. You don't have to be fancy and super technical. It's much better to focus on being clear with your words than trying to come up with a clever line or phrase.

What's more important is testimonials. Remember testimonials are key at this point because the prospect has unlikely spoken to you or met you before and as a result would like reassurance you're the real deal. Despite the fact you've got a great offer and you understand exactly what they need, some people still want to ensure they're making a good decision to book an appointment. This is where testimonials come in.

All you have to do is simply ask existing patients and clients to do a quick video testimonial for you whilst they're in the office otherwise it's unlikely they'll do it on their own time. The testimonial only has to be 2 minutes long and the patient or client simply has to talk about why they chose to do business with you in the first place and what result they gained from working with you. That's it. It doesn't need to be fancy. It just needs to communicate to prospective customers why a person did business with you and how successful the result is they received. I always recommend getting at least 3 video testimonials per treatment to put on each landing page.

Why You NEED Disclaimers in Your Testimonials & Why Failure to Do so Can be Catastrophic

The same process can be applied to written testimonials too. However the most important part about testimonials is you put a disclaimer at the bottom of the testimonials section to comply with Google's rules. Now Google may not ban you if you have a bad landing page but they'll give you a much lower quality score and as a result will affect your ability to rank nearly as highly as you could for the keywords you want to bid on. You'll want to use this disclaimer:

> "Results in each testimonial may not be typical and aren't the same for each patient/client. Results do vary".

Some of you may disagree and say you'll put a lot of people off with saying that.

But…

1. You'll build more trust for being honest with people doing that.

2. You're also following Google's policies so they rank you in a higher position so you have more chance in converting more patients anyway.

That's all you need to know about testimonials. Let's now discuss a little conversion rate optimization and where you want to put enquiry forms and call buttons on your pages to ensure your pages convert at the highest percentage possible. You may be thinking well isn't a great offer and quality copy enough for people to convert? Yes that will be enough for some people to convert but remember when I mentioned about making life easy for prospects…? That's what we're doing with placing buttons strategically on the page. So as you can see below in figure 18.6 where the button to call the office is. It's right in front of the actual offer which makes it so simple and easy for a person to call in right there. You're not in the business of making anything difficult for potential patients and clients.

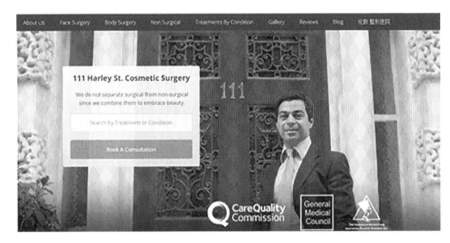

Figure 18.6 showing a good call to action in a great position on a landing page.

The reason we're keeping it easy is because we have a bias in our brain called the availability bias. We humans tend to make decisions extremely quickly without rational thought and most of our decisions are made from these cognitive biases in our brain. There's 25+ of them and you can research this a little more by watching this video by the great Charlie Munger who did a talk at a college going through 25 of them: https://www.youtube.com/watch?v=pqzcCfUglws

The point is you can lose upwards of 25% of quality enquiries by not positioning the button and form above the fold of your landing page.

Even when a person scrolls down the landing page they should still always be able to click a button to call right in because what happens if they scroll down the page and want to take action and there's no button? You think they're going to scroll right back up the page again…?

Well the majority of people will leave the page right then and there because their brain makes the quick decision it takes too much energy to scroll up the page again to call you. Seriously this may sound shallow but every single one of you reading has these cognitive biases in your brain and they influence your daily decisions. If you have to make your prospect think about how to take action then you're wasting a lot of money. Plain and simply, be strategic with where you place your call to action buttons and your enquiries will be sure to go up as long as you've followed everything else I've explained to you in this chapter so far.

Now as we're nearing the end of this chapter I'm sure you're probably wondering how you'd even go about creating landing pages in the first place. Well that's a great question. The easiest way is to instruct the agency you're working with to build out a landing page for you which follows the same structure I've laid out here even though they'll explain their landing pages are better. That's your decision of who you want to believe but if you're not acquiring the amount of quality patients & clients you want every month then it might be better to follow my advice. If you're sick and tired of the agencies you've worked with and want to build the landing page yourself then you can follow this way I'm about to show you.

One of the easiest ways you can build a landing page yourself is if you have a wordpress based site. You'll know what type of site you have simply by asking your web developer. If you don't have a wordpress site then I'd strongly recommend you switching over to a wordpress site. (That doesn't mean you need a brand new site by the way). All you have to do then as you can see below in figure 18.7, is click on pages on the right hand side of the dashboard and then as you can see in figure 18.8 click on the duplicate button under the best page you want to use. I'm telling you to duplicate an existing page which is relevant because it'll be much quicker for you to edit that one and change the content than simply creating a brand new page. Once you've done that you're ready to go.

Figure 18.7 showing how to access your pages in Wordpress.

Figure 18.8 showing how you can duplicate pages in Wordpress.

You simply have to edit the page by writing in the specific message you want and position the buttons on your page in the right place. Once you've done that you've made a landing page better than 95% of landing pages agencies make for business owners.

Now we've finished this chapter we can move onto the importance of retargeting/remarketing and building audiences. This is a skill just like anything else and is surprisingly simple to master. Let's dive into it right now. Are you ready?

Chapter 19

Your Best Competitors
Stalk Your Customers

————— ♦ —————

Okay so we're at the point right now where I've thrown a lot of information at you. You're in a great position at this point because you simply have to absorb the information and then apply it.

Now we can start to move onto more advanced strategies to increase the amount of quality patients you're acquiring from Google Adwords. These strategies themselves won't make or break your campaign like Clickfraud technology, quality score or copy will but they certainly will prevent you from losing easy patients and clients you should've acquired. So let's dive into this.

What is Retargeting & Why is it so Important to the Success of Your Adwords Campaigns?

Retargeting is simply a small piece of code every single Google account has which you put on your website and landing page and then show an ad to people who've not taken a specific action. For example you retarget people who haven't opted into the form you have on your landing page as they showed interest in what you're offering.

You're not violating any terms and conditions because these people already showed interest in your offer. If you qualify people properly in your ad copy and it's very clear what you have to offer then a person won't click on it unless they're at least somewhat interested.

So why is retargeting important? It's very important because in the modern world as I said before there's always something or multiple things tugging at a person's attention. As a result it becomes very difficult for a person to keep focused on your ad especially when other things they prioritise can jump in the way and take your prospect's attention again. So what's the point in missing out on these perfectly great prospects when you could simply retarget them with your offer again?

You're not being needy when you're offering high value. Some of you at this point may think well it's a waste of money if people are clicking our ads and then not taking any action as a result. To that I'd say well if retargeting cost a lot then I'd agree with you. But as you're not bidding on any particular keyword and instead you're advertising based off an audience then it's very cheap. You'd be surprised at how cheap it is to run very successful retargeting ads. So understand retargeting is one of the key areas where you can spend $100 and make back $10,000 because it costs so little to show ads to highly interested people in the first place.

The Brutal Consequences of Failing to Use Retargeting

At this point many of you may be thinking well what happens if I don't decide to do retargeting? It's not a bad question. Well it's going to take longer for you to see a higher return on investment because people get so distracted in the modern world it's difficult to expect people to take action off the first touch of your ad. As a result your level of frustration will build because you're not doing badly but you could be doing so much better.

What makes it even worse is the people who you don't retarget will simply forget about you (not on purpose) and find someone else who is at the top of their mind. Remember, retargeting creates the top of mind effect and the longer you can stay at the top of a person's mind the higher chance they'll give you a call. If a person only sees your ad once then how are you supposed to stay top of mind of your ideal patients and clients…?

Advanced Retargeting from Google to Facebook

Now let's move onto something a little more advanced. I've spoken in one of the early chapters about how to place your Google remarketing code onto your website and as a result your landing page. Now let's talk about your Facebook retargeting code in addition to your Adwords campaigns. So retargeting on Google is great but we can take it one step further. Despite the fact Google is best for finding patients and clients who are in greatest need right now, Facebook still has 1.3 billion daily users which means if a person is searching on Google for a solution of yours chances are they're on Facebook too. So what can we do?

Well many of you already have a Facebook page for your business and if you don't then I strongly recommend you get one here:

https://www.facebook.com/business/learn/set-up-facebook-page

Once you've done that you want to sign up to what's called Facebook Business Manager which I spoke about heavily in my first book "The Facebook Advertising Solution". Firstly, go to: https://www.business.facebook.com and you'll come to a page which looks like figure 19.1 below. Simply sign up with your personal Facebook email which is connected to your personal Facebook account and then you'll go into the home screen of the business manager.

Figure 19.1 showing the Facebook Business Manager sign up page.

Now you've done that go to the top left hand side of your screen as you can see below in figure 19.2 and look for the option which says "Pixels". Click on that and if you haven't set up a pixel which most of you haven't I've made a quick video right here and how to set up a pixel and where to place the tracking code on any wordpress site. If you don't have a wordpress site then ask your web developer to do it for you. They'll know what you mean.

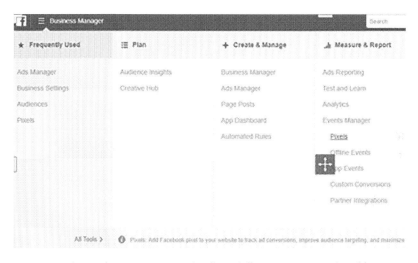

Figure 19.2 shows how to access the "Pixels" option in Facebook's Business manager.

Watch the short video here:
https://www.youtube.com/watch?v=_xBUKOqgXSE

Once you've done this, you're going to want to create the right audience off your pixel to ensure the right people see your retargeting ad on Facebook. The last thing you want is the wrong people to see your ad and then have lots of complaints about advertising to people who have no relevance to what you're offering. Once you've found the tab on the left hand menu "Audiences" you want to click:

1. Create Audience.

2. Then click the option Website Traffic.

3. Then under website Visitors you'll want to click the option "People who visited Specific web pages".

4. Once you've done that copy and paste the URL/Link of your landing page into the box.

5. Then on the right hand side of the screen you will see an option which says "Exclude More"as you can see in figure 19.3.

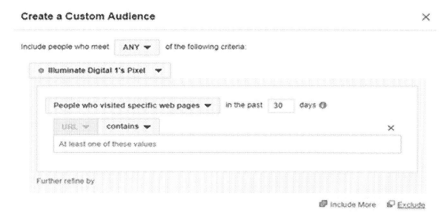

Figure 19.3 showing how to exclude people from your retargeting audience on Facebook.

1. Click that and then change the option of website traffic to "People who visited Specific web pages" again.

2. Then copy and paste the URL/link when a person puts their details into the form and submits it. (The URL will be different when a person hasn't submitted the form and after they've submitted the form.)

Now you've set the audience up, I've created a short video once more on how you can set up the actual Ad itself to run on Facebook optimally. As that's quite a long process to put in book form I've created an *unlisted video only for the readers of this book.* You can get the video right here:

https://www.youtube.com/watch?v=7TL2GlR2FmQ

So you're now in the position where you're retargeting people on both Google & Facebook which is costing you pennies in the process. To retarget successfully on both platforms you can budget $50-$200 a month at the most depending on how many visitors click your ad and come to your site.

As a result you're hitting people from 2 different angles which means it's much easier for your business to stay top of mind because your ideal patients and clients can't help but constantly see you. Marvellous right? What makes this process even better is barely any business does this. It's somewhat scary to think these tools are there for people to use yet they don't use them. You're not like most business owners. Instead you might implement these tools which is going to benefit you far more than trusting an "expert" agency to do the job for you.

As I said before this stuff and content here isn't rocket science. Anyone can learn it and start to implement it. It's just most agencies and business owners either don't know about it or they have some idea of it and simply don't implement it into their current marketing. As a result this ruins the new amount of quality patients/clients and referrals you can get out of your existing marketing every single month. Having more tools in your tool belt makes this process so much easier. No one likes to feel limited.

Anyway now you know these advanced strategies, let's start to talk about the importance of testing in the next chapter. One of the main factors you'll learn is testing isn't necessarily important because of the skill aspect but more the way you think about testing as a whole which will yield the best results for your practice. Let's dive into it right now!

Chapter 20

Your Chances of Success are in Direct Proportion to the Amount of Tests You Run

———◆———

Now we all know humans are naturally lazy right? It's simply in our nature to try and do the least amount of effort possible whilst maximising gain as much as possible. There isn't that much wrong with this in the broad spectrum of things because obviously time management is key.

But the issue arises when you try and do as little work as possible on the extremely important tasks such as testing. It's one of the only tasks with regard to online marketing which business owners and agencies don't really like doing because it can get repetitive for most people. However repetitive doesn't mean unimportant. If anything the difference between success and failure is doing the important tasks over and over again to a high level which are the same tasks other people don't want to do.

Why is Testing Your Ads so Dam Important?

Well it's very important because if you don't do it you're trying to guess what works and what doesn't. How are you supposed to guess what works and what doesn't if you have no data to back your theories up?!?! As a result once you have data in from your initial ads you can start to find out what works, what doesn't and what works best. Now of course later in this chapter we're going to talk specifically about how to test with regard to Google Adwords but as I said your mindset must be right before we move on to that.

You must remove the toxic belief of you put up an ad, test a few times or don't test at all and then you're done. Nothing could be further from the truth.

You simply cannot expect to put up a few ads for different services and expect success because people's problems are changing all the time which means you have to change along with it. You must adapt. If you're at one moment solving a specific problem for people and then the same problem changes which it will, you're now behind the curve meaning less people want to work with you because you've failed to understand the new core problem the person is experiencing.

Why Can't I Just Test My Own "Logical" Theories?

For example the initial problem for people in America back in the early 1900s was finding a faster way of moving around other than walking. Of course horses and buggies were used extensively. Then Henry Ford figured out there was a different problem at large. Horses were simply too slow and weren't moving fast enough for people to get to the position they wanted to. As a result he came up with the idea of Ford Motors which solved the problem of saving people dramatically more time.

Now just imagine Henry Ford had simply created another version of a horse and buggy. It wouldn't have solved the new fundamental problem at large which was saving people's time. As a result he'd of appeared just like any other commodity. So this is the reason you can't just write ads and do little to no testing. You have to test what resonates best with potential patients and clients in your market you want to target. If you don't test, these prospects likely aren't going to be enticed enough to come in for some kind of consultation again which means you're in the position of wasting more money on advertising.

The moral? You must constantly be testing and making decisions based off the data you have rather than any theories you've come up with. More often that not the theory which you're so sure will work often doesn't work nearly as well as you think it could've which of course sucks because you had such high expectations of what was going to work. Instead you're going to look at the data and make informed decisions of what message or angle to test next because you know already what's working and what isn't working. You've literally got proof right in front of you of what's working and what isn't and we're going to dive into how to structure tests right now for Google Adwords.

Now you're in the position where you understand the importance of testing. You don't make decisions based off your theory or judgement of what can work and instead make decisions off the data in front of you. On top of which you also understand the importance of continual testing and your new refusal of simply putting an ad on the internet and doing little to no testing of it.

How Do I Start Split Testing More Effectively?

So how long are your average tests supposed to last for? Well I can tell you a good time with Google Adwords is between 2-3 days. I say 2-3 days because for some of you in very large cities such as NYC, LA, Chicago etc are going to have a much higher volume of people to work with and as a result data will come in faster. Smaller cities such as Boston, Sacramento, Orlando, Miami etc will need roughly 3-5 days to see the results of what's worked and what hasn't in a test.

Now I will say before you do go in and test, ensure as you can see in figure 20.1 below you have the option "Rotate Ads Indefinitely" turned on.

The reason I'm telling you this is because you want each ad you test to have the same exposure as an ad which is already working. This is because if your tests get very little exposure compared to the performing ad being optimised, the test wasn't particularly fair because it didn't get the exposure it needed to know if the copy worked or not. As a result make sure your ads are set to this option rather than being set to "optimized" otherwise your tests will likely go down the toilet in terms of effectiveness.

Figure 20.1 showing how to set your ads to "Rotate Indefinitely".

With Google Adwords as a whole the main form of testing you'll be doing is copy and to be more specific:

1. Headline 1.

2. Headline 2.

3. Display URL.

4. Ad description.

5. Your Landing page.

Your first thought might be, "Dam that's a lot to test". Well it really isn't because you can successfully find a high performing angle of every single one of these components by the end of 30 days. This is the reason I always recommend a business owner give an agency 60 days because sometimes it does take 60 days to find a message which works best for your market.

So where do we start? Well we want to start with headline 1 and once we've found a particular headline which works really well then we can move onto headline 2. The reason we're testing one angle at a time is because otherwise how are you supposed to know what succeeded in a test and what didn't? If you test both headlines, your description and landing pages all at the same time you may get a lot of conversions but you don't know what is causing those conversions and when conversions slow down you won't know what needs to be changed and optimized. So always test one angle at a time.

Now, you want to have 3 different variations of the same ad with changes to the angle you're testing. I choose 3 because 2 isn't enough variations and 4 variations can hurt how much traffic you can comfortably test to run a fair and valid test. Plus with 3 different variations it gives you a nice amount of information to be able to take onto the next test which is very important. You build on each test as you go along rather than extracting little data out of each test and failing to progress well.

Remember progression is key in testing. Once we've figured out we moving in a good direction on one angle then we can move onto the next angle. So at this point, some of you might be asking how do you create multiple ads per ad group? Great question. As you can see in figure 20.2 all you have to do is go to your Campaign, then select the Ad group you want to test (you should be testing on all ad groups at the same time), click on "Ads" at the top and then you'll be brought to the same page as figure 20.2. Now you can click the red button and create more ads to the same ad group.

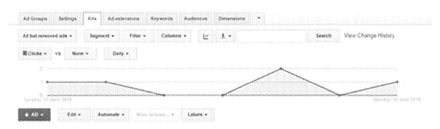

Figure 20.2 showing how you can click the red button to create more ads in the same ad group.

So as I said before, we test headline 1 first and keep everything else the same. Once you've tested headline 1, you've now got a strong baseline to move from and the goal with testing each angle is by the end of 30 days to have a strong baseline ad on all the angles I've mentioned above to test brand new ads against. The baseline ad you create may seem obvious at the end but has likely taken you at least 3 weeks to reach that point. Just so you know, most agencies and business owners never reach this point.

Now many of you may be thinking well how am I supposed to know what has worked better besides an increase in phone calls and enquires? Well you can look at these different metrics each time to know if one ad has outperformed another:

1. More phone calls have come in and you can see the phone calls tracked on Call Rail or some other third party software.

2. More patients and clients have come through your front door and you know for a fact what advertising medium they've come from.

3. Your Click through Rate is higher meaning one of your ads has been clicked on more in comparison to the amount of people who've seen the ad.

4. You've received more clicks.

Now remember the best metric is of course more patients coming through the door but that doesn't always happen especially when you're on a lower budget and are just starting out with a brand new ad account. As a result you've got to be able to use other pieces of data to determine which ads have been more successful than other ads. As I've said over and over again, your situation of starting out with a new ad account is going to be very different from a friend of yours who is doing very well on Adwords.

Often times people have spent 5+ figures to get their ad account to the point where they're ranking in position 1 in the first place and it's unlikely you want to do that. Instead testing is key especially strategic testing.

So what happens when a test doesn't work? All you would do is turn the ad off. I wouldn't recommend deleting the ad because it's information which you'll need going forward of what hasn't worked. You don't want to run another test of the same thing if it's already proven not to work.

On top of which many of you may be thinking well won't it be difficult to know if clicks have gone up each time on every test because surely the data from the previous ad would add onto the next test...? Well fortunately for you every angle you change in an ad, the data resets which is one of the reasons I suggest creating new ads for new tests because you have all your account history with your old ads of what doesn't work.

Trust me *the difference between testing well and testing badly is having a strong idea of what has worked so far & what has failed.* If you aren't keeping some track of what has failed then how are you supposed to progress forward?

Why You Must Forge the Mindset of "Never Stop Testing"

I thought so. Now the final point to this chapter is a mindset shift which you're going to find extremely valuable. Many of you after reading this chapter may think, well once you've found your baseline you can stop testing and leave the ad running because it's working right? Yes of course it's working but one thing is for sure is it will:

1. Eventually stop working leaving you in a situation where you've got to start heavy testing again.

2. There is almost always another variation of the same ad which works better than the one you're having success with right now. That's a guarantee.

As a result you must keep testing. You've done all the heavy lifting of finding a baseline which is bringing you at least a 700% ROI using all the strategies in this book but you can't stop testing now.

Eventually the ad doing very well for you as I've said before will stop working or at least not work nearly as well. So understand there's always a variation of the same ad which works better and all you have to do is find out what it is and you can only find out what it is through relentless testing. This is one of the reasons very few people can say they have enormous success every year with their advertising as a local business (At least 1000% ROI) because either they or the agency they've hired doesn't want to keep testing.

Testing is a year round commitment and even if you're the 1 in a 1000 case where you've found an ad which can't be improved then you still don't want to assume this. You want to assume there's always a better version of what you have now. If your current baseline is producing a 700% ROI then assume you can find a version which will produce a 1000% ROI.

But you'll never find it unless you constantly test new angles.

How do you think companies triple and quadruple their businesses in a year...? It comes from testing new marketing messages every single day constantly trying to improve on what works. They leave their current ads which are working alone and separately come up with new ads trying to beat it. This is part of the game of Google Adwords. Always trying to beat your previous best and when you start playing this game you'll get so addicted your business can't help but keep growing. Either get addicted to the game of Google Adwords or find someone who is because the companies who never stop testing are the ones who stay on top of the hottest trends, win the most business and as a result dominate their market.

If you loved this chapter you're most certainly going to love the next one. It's very likely in your Google Advertising you're going to run into some obstacles and your campaigns will stall. As I said before this will happen unless you're on top of it and know how to get out of these obstacles. Let's discuss this right now.

Chapter 21

Don't Let Your
Campaigns Die

———◆———

We're nearing the end of this book but it's critical we talk about one topic which kills almost all Adwords campaigns in the end. That principle is not understanding how to deal with issues which will arise in your campaign regardless of how successful you've been so far. For many reasons which we'll talk about in this chapter, your campaigns can do extremely well for 4 months and then one day your conversions drop completely and you start seeing near to no enquiries and phone calls. How does that work…?

Reason 1 = Low Quality Score

Well one of the biggest reasons I see is businesses who try to outspend everyone on Google without high quality copy, good landing pages or account management. What normally happens is because the quality score usually isn't that great it's very easy for competitors to come in with much better copy and quality score, Google sees this and prefers this ad over yours because of the higher relevance. Remember Google are in business to make money but they're not going to make lots of money at the expense of their users who might complain and leave. Google has competitors just like you do and they can't afford to annoy their users. This is why I never recommend just trying to outspend your competition because you leave yourself in a very vulnerable position to lose position 1.

So how do I even look and access quality score? That's a great question. All your have to do is simply move your mouse over the text part of the keyword on each ad as you can see below in figure 21.1 and then the quality score will pop right up. You'll also be able to see the factors within your quality score and which ones are doing well and which ones are below average. As I said before most of the time your issue with your campaigns will be your quality score and that's fine because there's simple fixes which you can implement right now.

Keyword: **foundation repair los angeles**

Displaying ads right now?

> Yes

Quality Score - Learn more

> 7/10   Expected click-through rate: **Average**
> Ad relevance: **Above average**
> Landing page experience: **Average**

Ad Preview and Diagnosis

Figure 21.1 showing the factors you can use to improve your quality score.

You have 3 factors within quality score which I've already mentioned in previous chapters such as:

1. Relevance.

2. Landing pages.

3. Your click through rate.

So how do you improve these? Well let's start with relevance. The easiest thing you can do right away is by ensuring your keyword is the first part of your headline, ensure your keyword is inserted inside of your description copy and display URL to be sure. Once you've done this, check the keywords you're bidding on.

You could easily be bidding on keywords which are irrelevant to what you're offering i.e. you bid on [coffee mugs] when in reality you're just selling mugs. It's very surprising how many businesses make these simple mistakes and end up having a terrible quality score in the process. That's all you need to do with regards to relevance.

Now landing pages are a big one simply because there is more to go wrong. You don't just have copy to be wary of but also specific pictures, testimonials etc. On top of which Google doesn't specifically tell you what's wrong with your landing pages except drop your quality score. You have to figure it out which is the reason I'm going to give you a mini checklist to ensure every single landing page of yours does these things:

1. Does your landing page have the main keyword I.e. Breast Augmentation Austin on it? This doesn't mean you have to completely overload your landing page with the keyword but it does mean your keyword must be inserted at least once on your page.

2. Ensure you aren't using naked women or women with personal body parts showing because Google will hurt you heavily for this.

3. Ensure all of your testimonials have the mini disclaimer beneath them I.e. "Results vary and aren't the same for every patient."

4. Make sure you have an up to date privacy policy and terms of conditions on your website and landing page. It amazes me how many businesses have a privacy policy and terms of conditions which is out of date . In California, NYC, Florida etc you can be fined $10,000 minimum if you're reported. Who wants to take that risk...?

That's it. Like I said before it's not rocket science but you just have to implement these things onto your pages. As I've said many times before, the successful people simply do the things the unsuccessful people refuse to do. So when it comes to quality score and success with Google Adwords, it largely comes down to balancing being in line with Google's rules whilst ensuring potential patients and client's want to work with you. No one gets enticed by boring copy even if you're super in line with Google's terms of service.

Last thing in improving your quality score is click through rate. The easiest way to increase your click through rate is to improve the quality of your copy. So how do you do that? Simple. If people aren't responding to your ad meaning your calls are low and your click through rate is low then you know the issue is with your ad copy not your landing page. If your landing page was the issue your CTR would be relatively high because people liked your ad but didn't convert from your landing page. So firstly if people aren't responding to your ad you:

1. Haven't got the core desires right the person wants.

2. Haven't phrased these desires in the right way for a person to understand.

So how do you deal with these? Well first off you must understand before you do any advertising the core desires you're looking to entice out of the person in the first place. Therefore if your ad isn't working you must already be testing the same desires just phrased in a different way. If 3 different variations of the same ad hasn't worked then it's very likely you've got the desires wrong. Remember a person responds based off how well you frame your offer to their deepest desires and if you haven't framed your offer to their deepest desires then why should they respond…? They have no incentive to.

On top of which a person doesn't see your offer through logic. Just because you see your offer as the logical choice for specific types of people doesn't mean they view it with the same logic. Instead they view your offer through the lens of their own desires and if you don't meet their desires then they won't respond to your offer. Simple. As a result you must go back to the drawing board and ask patients the reason they really took a specific treatment with you and go from there.

I will say though often times a person won't tell you the most vulnerable intangible reasons they took your service. Instead they'll tell you a good justification such as, it was "Great value for money" or "Super experienced surgeon/doctor/attorney" etc. Therefore you must listen carefully for the emotion behind the words of the person and then go from there. Remember the emotional drive for a person to take action is much greater than the logical one. *The emotional drive gets the person ready to take your offer and the logical drive gets the person to move.* But a person will never move if they don't have an emotional reason to move in the first place.

Reason 2 = Not Spending Enough a.k.a. Fear of Overspending

Now interestingly enough, a big reason people's campaigns don't get moving in the first place is because they aren't willing to spend enough. I know I said clickfraud technology will reduce your ad spend by at least 3-7 times what you would have to spend without it but that doesn't mean you can be cheap and expect big results. Remember the businesses who acquire the most customers most of the time are the ones who spend the most money. Now I didn't say that was the best way at all but businesses do it because it's a much easier way than learning how to do it properly. Heck people who bought this book probably gave up and opted to go that route.

So as you can see below in figure 21.2 what happens when you don't put up a big enough bid in the first place for your ad to show high enough in the rankings. It simply says your ad can't show high enough because you haven't been willing to put up the budget to compete. Now the difference between you and most businesses however is whilst you both put up the same high bid you'll end up spending much less as a result whereas the business just trying to win by outspending will have to pay that enormous bid. Just because you bid $200 for a keyword doesn't mean you'll spend that much. It's just simply the amount *you're prepared to spend not how much you will spend*. Don't forget this the next time you're scared of putting up a super high number to start your bidding for a keyword.

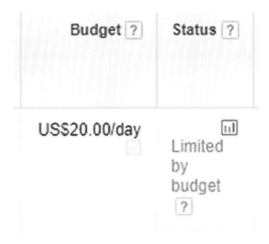

Figure 21.2 showing what happens when you don't bid enough for the keywords you're advertising on.

So far all of these issues have been relatively simple to deal with. The final obstacle you'll likely run into is having low impressions. This is an obstacle virtually every single brand new account has when first starting out on Google which isn't a fun time. Remember as I said before, every new account gets put into a sandbox which means Google limits the amount of people (impressions) who get to see your ad because they don't yet trust you enough. Don't worry. There's a few ways out of it:

1. Raise your click through rate which the easiest way is by improving your ad copy.

2. Increasing the amount you're willing to bid on your keywords.

3. Improve your quality score which I've gone over a few pages back and dedicated and entire chapter on how to improve your quality score.

Google can clearly be a pain at times but once you know how to deal with every single obstacle they throw at you you'll approach Adwords with a much higher level of confidence. Understand most businesses approach Adwords with a lottery ticket mindset meaning once they find a few ads which work really well and put them in position 1 they can sit back and relax.

As I spoke about in the testing chapter earlier, you can never sit back and relax with Adwords and this is the reason most business owners outsource their work to external agencies. This doesn't work 95% of the time because most agencies aren't highly skilled in everything surrounding Adwords we've gone over so far and as a result can't consistently provide the results. Therefore you will run into obstacles with Adwords regardless of how well your campaigns are doing right now. The key is to understand these obstacles are heading your way and know exactly how to deal with them. Then it's very unlikely you'll stop winning.

Next we're going to talk about an extremely important factor in Adwords success. What do you think will happen if you're running Adwords campaigns and the account isn't managed and organised properly? What can you imagine going wrong if you account has poor organisation? That's what we're going to talk about next.

Chapter 22

Granular Account Organisation

———————◆———————

Have you ever considered organisation in your account is extremely important to your success on the front end of Adwords? Well it's extremely important. Most people don't know how important. Business owners wonder how they heck they spend thousands of dollars on Adwords a month and it just seems to go so fast.

Understand, your budget only went fast because you weren't monitoring it. It's the exact same with your finances. If you don't have an accountant/s or someone to manage where your money goes then of course you're going to wonder how money is leaving your account so fast. Well here is something important for you to understand, the minute you fully recognise exactly where each dollar is being spent on Adwords you'll often times spend more than you initially intended because you know how well your campaigns are doing.

You haven't left your budget in the dark. Instead you're openly managing it and understanding exactly where it's going inside of your account. Budget is just the beginning of granular account organisation which is a term from Brad Geddes fantastic book "Advanced Google

Adwords" which relates to you organising your keywords into the right ad groups. The better you get with keyword and ad group organisation the better you'll be able to manage your budget and that's something we're going to discuss right now.

The Most Effective Way to Structure Your Ad Groups

As you can see below in figure 22.1, a picture of various different ad groups lined up for an orthodontist client I've recently started working with. One of the main services we're advertising for is Invisalign so I immediately separated all orthodontist based keywords from Invisalign keywords. Why did I do that? I did that because I want to keep relevance as high as possible because if your relevance is low it's going to impact your quality score and as a result reduce your ability to be in position 1 for the most important keywords you're going after. You can also see I've separated orthodontist city based keywords from each other too. For example I'm not going to put *"Orthodontist NYC"* in the same ad group as *"Orthodontist Brooklyn"*. Again it all comes down to relevance and having the highest relevance possible.

+ AD GROUP		Edit ▾	Details ▾	Bid strategy ▾	Automate ▾
☐	●	Ad group	Status [?]	Default Max CPC [?]
☐	●	Orthodontist Columbia SC	Eligible	US$20.00 (enhanced)
☐	●	Invisalign Columbia SC	Eligible	US$10.00 (enhanced)
☐	●	Orthodontist Lexington SC	Eligible	US$20.00 (enhanced)
☐	‖	Straighten teeth	Paused	US$15.00 (enhanced)
☐	●	Braces in Lexington SC	Eligible	US$15.00 (enhanced)

Figure 22.1 showing granular account organisation with keywords.

193

So when in doubt look at the similarity of each keyword you're going after I.e. Invisalign NYC, Braces NYC, Orthodontist NYC, Orthodontist Brooklyn etc and only include keywords in these ad groups if they have very similar words in them. That's what granular account organisation is. You should never have Invisalign keywords in the same ad group as braces keywords. They're completely different words and as a result will ruin your relevance.

RELATED KEYWORDS REPORT 1 - 100 (235)

Keyword	Related %	Volume	KD	CPC (USD)
denver personal injury lawyer	85.00	720	54.33	174.03
denver injury lawyer	85.00	260	53.49	237.39
personal injury lawyer denver co	85.00	210	56.76	144.27
personal injury attorney denver co	80.00	390	59.86	183.21
denver injury attorney	80.00	170	55.58	226.12
injury attorneys in denver	75.00	40	59.09	0.00
personal injury denver	75.00	20	55.97	72.23
denver personal injury law firms	70.00	140	50.83	219.51
best injury lawyer in denver	65.00	50	57.96	0.00
best personal injury lawyer denver	65.00	20	52.51	97.26
Remove info	60.00	30	59.05	0.00

Figure 22.2 showing lots of variations of keywords for "personal injury attorney denver".

As a result you want to plan before you run your campaigns and start implementing keywords, it's a great idea to have a look at all the different keywords to understand how many ad groups you can create from the keywords you have available. For example, as you can see down in figure 22.2 the different types of keyword variations I have for a personal injury attorney in Denver Colorado. I could create:

1. Personal Injury Attorney Denver.

2. Personal Injury Lawyer Denver.

3. Denver Injury Attorney.

4. Best Injury Lawyer in Denver.

5. Best Personal Injury Lawyer Denver.

That's just off these keywords. I haven't even gone into the keyword planner to find problem based and symptom based keywords either. You can clearly see what I'm doing here. I'm separating every single difference I can see becoming an issue if I put the keyword in the same ad group.

For example many of you might object because I didn't put *"Denver injury attorney"* in the same ad group as *"Personal injury attorney Denver"*. It's a small difference but it's still important you separate the keywords to avoid any possibility of Google ruining your relevance which obviously you don't want to happen. We want Google on our side as much as possible.

How Can I Best Structure My Keywords?

Now some of you may be wondering, well how many keywords do I put in an ad group? What keywords can I put in the same ad group? I spoke about this earlier in the keyword chapter so I'll show you the best way to do this. Firstly, it's not particularly a good idea to just have one keyword per ad group because Google will penalise you for this. They'll come up with a very rational reason you can't do this when in reality they know they'll make far more money when you have multiple keywords per ad group. So follow this. I personally would recommend a minimum of 5 keywords per ad group especially when you have very few options for keywords. However for most of you, 10 keywords per ad group is ideal and if you fall between 5-10 keywords that's fine also.

So as you can see below in figure 22.3 the different types of keywords which you can put in the same ad group. For example you can have *personal injury attorney denver, denver personal injury attorney, denver personal injury attorneys* etc in the same ad group because there isn't going to be a relevance issue. You know right away when you write your copy there isn't going to be a problem in terms of your copy clashing with the keywords you've decided to bid on in the same ad group.

Figure 22.3 showing similar keywords in one ad group.

However lets say you were super limited on variations then it wouldn't be the worst idea to throw *personal injury attorney denver* in the same ad group as *injury attorney denver*. But the only time you can do this is when you're extremely limited on the keywords you can put in your ad group. It's better to risk this than to have 1-3 keywords in your ad group and Google punish you by either raising your costs, showing your ads to less people etc.

That's granular account organisation in a nutshell. One point it's important for me to make is the importance of you going into your account every day or 2 to check on tests, budget management etc. You don't want to check once a week because you could easily spend $5,000 extremely quickly simply by not paying attention. Even agencies running your account for you, it would make sense for you to check in on the work they're doing to check how they're spending your money.

How the Pros Organise their Account

The point is the minute you lose organisation of your account is the minute you lose control of how well you're going to do with Adwords. Frankly if you really don't want to run your own Adwords and just want to know the theory, I'd recommend hiring someone else and checking in on the account every few days or so to see what they're doing. At least this way you have the knowledge to know if they're doing a good job or not.

Just because new patients are coming through the door doesn't mean a good job is being done. If you had to spend $1,000 into Adwords yet you got a $1,500 customer, you've got overhead and everything else on top, your profit and ROI isn't particularly good.

A great example is a client of mine down in Orlando thought he was getting really great SEO work done but in reality the company completely messed up his entire brand's security and he had no idea. My mentor who I referred over had to spend over 5 months fixing all the brand damage the company had done. Had my client had the knowledge of SEO, he'd of known how terrible of a job they were doing.

It's the exact same with Google Adwords and your practice. If you don't know how everything works, how to write above average copy then you're not going to know if not only a good job is being done but also who to hire next because you won't be able to tell who's telling the truth or not. The moral? Learn to be constantly paying attention to the work which is being done on your behalf. You've been warned.

How much easier would it be for you if you could get your own reports from your Adwords campaigns instead of relying on people to send them to you? Well that's exactly what we're going to dive into the next chapter. Let's jump into it right now!

Chapter 23

Reporting & Analysing
Data Like a Hero

———— ◆ ————

Reporting is one of the easiest ways for you to stay on top with regards to how well your campaigns are doing. As a result this chapter is going to show you exactly how to generate specific types of reports so you don't have to rely on your agency sending you them instead. Don't worry, it literally takes 60 seconds to generate your main campaign reports so it's not something you need any prior experience to do or learn to do.

The Different Metrics You Can Use in Your Reports to Reap Greater Adwords Success

First off how do you know from looking at the campaign data if your campaigns are improving, doing well or plain and simply need fixing? Well as you can see below in figure 23.1 the amount of options you can see to measure the success of your campaign. These options are just the tip of the iceberg to what else you can track. Now obviously Adwords gives you the default options but the one I would highly recommend you paying attention to is not only the amount of conversions you've received but also the cost per conversion. Your cost per conversion is everything because that's how much you're paying for a person to either submit a form on your landing page or acquire a phone call. The lower your cost per conversion the more money you're going to make because you're simply acquiring patients and clients at a much lower cost than most of your competitors.

Figure 23.1 showing the different metrics you can use to measure the success of your campaign.

As I mentioned in previous chapters, you don't just want to focus on how many clicks you're getting or how high your CTR is. Why am I saying this? The main reason for this is because those statistics can be very misleading because having a high CTR doesn't mean many of those prospects are converting. Just like having a lot of clicks doesn't mean those clicks are converting into actual patients and clients. As a result don't get so stressed out about how good your CTR is or how many clicks you're getting and instead focus more on the amount of conversions you're getting and the cost per conversion.

Now I'm not saying CTR and clicks aren't important metrics because they are in terms of helping you know if a test has been more successful as mentioned in a previous chapter. What I'm saying is *it wouldn't be wise to determine whether your campaigns are succeeding based off CTR and clicks.* Seriously, once you start paying more attention to conversions in your campaign results you'll surprise yourself at how much better you become at acquiring more patients and clients through Google Adwords in general.

Now let's talk about generating reports of your own. Just so you know most agencies will send reports and heavily focus on CTR and clicks because any campaign can be disguised as doing well by having a half decent CTR and a half decent amount of clicks. This secretly hides the fact the campaigns aren't converting as well and therefore it's important you understand how to generate and read your own reports. Now you can do this in both Adwords and Google Analytics which is a bit more advanced so for now I'm going to show you how to generate reports purely in the Adwords home screen.

As you can see in figure 23.2 below, how simple it is to access your reporting within Adwords. You simply have to:

1. Click on "Reports" at the top of your screen.

2. Either click on the red report button or hover your mouse in figure 23.2 to see the various different reporting types.

3. Then simply select either "Campaign" as the report you want or any other specific factor you want to check up on.

Figure 23.2 showing how to generate a report from your Adwords campaign.

Once you've done that as you can see in figure 23.3 you have all of your data right in front of you with the option to download the data into a CSV file, Excel file etc which it's easy to email the report then to your colleagues if you'd like to do that. So why is reporting important?

Well it's important because it gives you a fantastic view of all the metrics for a specific timeline you want to check. So one of the easiest ways to determine a campaign's progression and success over a 90 day period is to check reports every single week, then compare every single month and then look at the data over a 90 day overview which you can also see in figure 23.4 on how to do that.

Once you've got a clear understanding of the direction your campaigns have been going it makes it so much easier to know what you want to do next. If you don't know this data then how are you supposed to know if your campaigns are going in the right direction? Simply seeing more patients and clients through the door isn't good enough to determine how well your campaigns are doing. For all I know your campaigns are doing well but how well in terms of statistical figures? Knowing this makes it so much easier to decide if you're going to keep working with the agency you've chosen or you're going to move on. Either way stay on top of this.

Reporting & Analysing Data Like a Hero

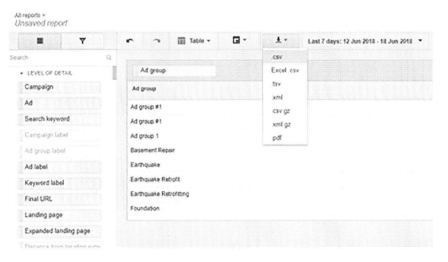

Figure 23.3 showing how to download a report you've generated.

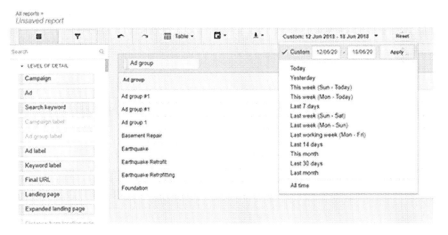

Figure 23.4 showing how to customise your reports to the date range you want.

Why are Keyword Reports so Important?

Now it's important we talk about keyword reports here because they're very important. Now so far we've spoken about campaign reports which are helpful for getting the general gist of how well your campaigns are doing. Now for most business owners that's going to be plenty enough to know statistically how well your campaigns are doing. But for those business owners who want to go a little deeper into the data of your campaigns then let's discuss keyword reports. So as you can see in figure 23.5 below how to generate a keyword report of your own and then add multiple other statistics I.e. CTR, Conversions, CPC etc to analyse every single keyword you're bidding on. You simply hover your mouse over predefined reports and generate one that way.

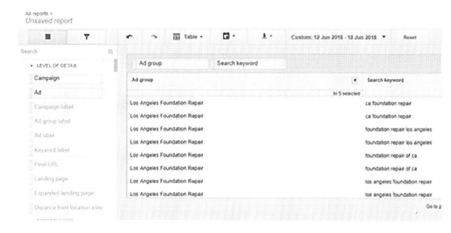

Figure 23.5 shows how to generate a keyword report.

So what's the importance of a keyword report? Well it's simple. Your Adwords success will largely come down to the keywords you not only decide to bid on initially but the keywords you decide to keep bidding on. If you keep bidding on the wrong keywords which aren't generating much for you then how are you supposed to know what keywords to optimise and double down on? The reason this is important is because most business owners will look at their home screen of Adwords and see how well a campaign is doing and when they click that they'll see how well their ad groups are doing. Yet business owners and even agencies for that matter rarely go deeper and check the keywords and even specific ads they're running to determine which ones are performing the best.

Remember as I've said before Google is going to spread your impressions around in your entire campaign because you need to have fair tests so you know which tests have been successful and which ones haven't. That's great in the beginning but it's important you're aware of the fact your impressions are going to get shared with every keyword so if you haven't gotten rid of the keywords which are under performing then the keywords which are working well for you don't get enough love.

As a result you won't acquire as many patients and client's as you could do because the best keywords and ads aren't getting the impressions they should be getting. As a result make sure to generate keyword reports every single week to stay on top of what keywords are working for you and which aren't. The keywords which aren't converting you simply turn them off as I've demonstrated in figure 23.6 for you below on how to do that. Remember, you test to figure out what works and you'll know what works based on the reports you generate. The keywords and ads which don't convert you turn off. The keywords and ads which do convert you double down on and put at the focus of your campaign. Simple.

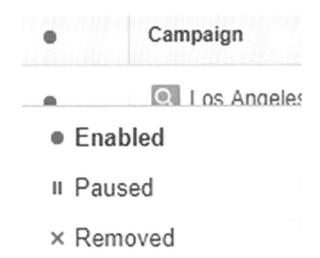

Figure 23.6 showing how to turn off campaigns.

Wow have I got a chapter for you next. So far throughout this book we've heavily focused on Google Adwords because it's the number 1 search engine in the entire world. As a result there are simply far more quality people who you can acquire for your business. Seems logical to start there as it offers the greatest opportunity. So the next chapter we're going to talk about the importance of Bing as a great compliment to Google once you've started to see great success with your Google Adwords campaigns. Seriously, even if you feel your Google campaigns are absolutely perfect and the agency you're working with is completely flawless then you'll get 10x more value from the Bing ads chapter alone. That's how important Bing is to scaling out your practice once you've built momentum with your Google Adwords campaigns. So without further ado, let's head face first into Bing right now.

Chapter 24

Bing Ads = 33%

———————◆———————

So we're here. This advertising platform is one of the most underused platforms a local business could use. The fact most businesses just use Adwords (not very well) and ignore Bing is the total ignorance of most ad agencies with regards to their clients.

The Importance & Underlying Purpose of Using Bing Ads in the 21st Century

Fact: every single business should be using Bing ads as along as Google Adwords is currently very successful for their business. Notice I didn't say use Bing ads if you've been successful on Google in the past and aren't currently successful. I said use Bing if you're presently having great success with Google.

Many of you may be wondering why in the world I put 33% as the title of this chapter…? Well it's a great question. Firstly understand Google is 66% of all search engine traffic meaning 66% of all searches on the internet are made through Google.

On the other side 33% of internet searches are made through Bing and a big reason for that is because a considerable amount of Microsoft computers come with Bing pre-installed and those people don't end up installing Google as their homepage instead. Personally I prefer Google but that doesn't mean 33% of all search engine users agree with me. Therefore if you're ignoring Bing you're missing out on an extra 33% of potential quality patients & clients which tangibly could be resulting in you losing millions of dollars simply because you haven't positioned your business on Bing. Imagine if you didn't advertise your local business on Google. You'd be considered silly for leaving Google out of your patient and client acquisition plan simply because of the amount of people who use it every single minute. So what's the point in leaving an extra 33% of internet searches off the table?

Well let's dive into this. Understand right away the purpose of Bing isn't to replace Google. At this current standpoint in late 2018, Google doesn't appear to be going anywhere in the foreseeable future. But who knows anything can happen. Therefore you always want to start on Google simply because you have double the amount of searches and potential patients and clients to start acquiring. DOUBLE!

Once you've cracked this and by cracked I mean you're achieving at least an 700% ROI every single month then you're in a great position to use Bing. (Yes 700% is very possible for every single business owner on Google providing they don't hire a bad agency which 97% of business owners do hire a bad one). Now you've established this you can move onto Bing as another advertising channel. Remember the man who chases 2 rabbits catches none. Therefore Bing is arguably the best compliment to Google simply because it's so similar in terms of the interface, targeting, budget to Google that it doesn't require an entire book to get Bing right.

The only thing I will say though is Bing tends to be used by the older generation which is roughly at this time people who are on average 50 years old & older. This means especially if you're a personal injury attorney you want to be using Bing because anyone at any age can get into an accident. Whereas a cosmetic surgeon may want to start slower with Bing because generally a lot of cosmetic surgery patients aren't 50+ unless you specialise with that age range. Hey that's a fantastic USP. The surgeon who only focuses on cosmetic surgery for those 50+. Interesting right…?

Your Optimal Bing Ads Strategy

Okay so let's talk strategy of Bing. You now understand the fundamental purpose of Bing and why it's important for almost every single business owner to start using it. What business owner can proudly say they're missing out on 33% of all search engine traffic? 1 in a million maybe. Anyway in terms of the interface as you can see below in figure 24.1, it looks extremely similar to Google. The reason it's very similar to Google is because it's another search engine & the best way to find your quality patients and clients is through keywords.

On top of which the reason I haven't recommend Facebook at this time is because of how different it is to Google and Bing and requires a completely separate book to discuss. It's an important source for quality leads and would recommend you checking it out once you've achieved success on Google first.

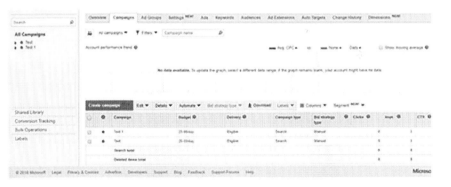

Figure 24.1 showing the Bing interface.

Super simple stuff so far right? Think of Bing as Google's baby brother except they're also competing against each other. So in terms of everything we've learned so far with Google I'm going to be talking about very similar things with Bing. So as you can see in figure 24.2 the objectives you can select when you decide to start your campaign from the Bing ads interface.

Now this is one of the few differences from Google because you don't really have campaign objectives with Google. Instead you only really can drastically change ad objectives I.e. Calls to your website, shopping ad, text ad etc. Therefore it's important you pay attention here.

Figure 24.2 showing Bing ads campaign objectives.

One of the first things you can do is import your Adwords campaigns from Google into Bing to cross compare results. The fact Bing is willing to do this tells you there should be no reason you shouldn't be using Bing. In order to do this as you can see below in figure 24.3, you go into your:

1. Campaign home screen.

2. Click "Import Campaigns" which is the 5th option to the right.

3. Then click "Import from Google Adwords".

Figure 24.3 showing how to import your Google campaigns into Bing.

Once you've done this you can now start your Bing campaigns with the best possible data to compare directly against. Remember, data is king and the more of it you have the better decisions you'll be able to make.

The Easiest Way to Structure Your Bing Campaigns

Now many of you haven't advertised on Bing before which once again means you're starting from scratch. Don't worry that's completely fine because you have to start from somewhere. It's better to start than to not start at all. Therefore this means you're going to have to start with:

1. "Visits to my website" which is another term for Clicks which is very similar to Facebook.

2. Once you've achieved a minimum of 30-50 conversions meaning phone calls and form submissions combined then you can use the campaign objective "Conversions in my website".

Almost identical to Facebook. You have to start with clicks because you need data quickly into your account and once you have enough conversions then you focus on the conversion objective completely. I know it's a pain that you've got to start over with these accounts but it's worth it in the long run.

As I've said before there will be the temptation to use the agency's account but what happens if you fall out with the agency? You've now spent all that money and you don't have any data to show for it so if you're going to spend money then make sure it's on your account even if it means you have to start from scratch.

Now you've set that up you can move onto targeting which you can see in figure 24.4 how similar this is to Adwords. I told you! It's really not too different from Adwords at all which makes it ever more easy to use this platform. It's not like I'm recommending you to advertise on a platform which is completely different to the one I've discussed for most of this book. Instead I'm recommending a search engine advertising platform which doesn't require much more skill to use. All that's required is an understanding of the few key differences. So use this link to decide which keywords you're going to go after and for most of you you're going to go after the exact same keywords as you're bidding on through Google:

https://advertise.bingads.microsoft.com/en-
gb/solutions/tools/keyword-planner

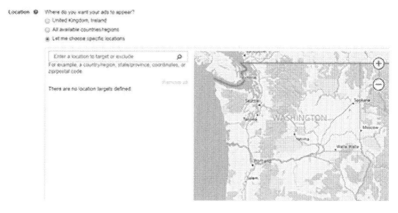

Figure 24.4 showing Targeting in Bing.

That's simply Bing's version of the Google keyword planner. Unfortunately they're aren't any good spy tools to search for keywords on Bing such as SEM Rush, Spyfu etc are for Google so you must use the Bing keyword planner. It's not a huge deal anyway considering most of you will be bidding on the same keywords as you're doing on Google anyway so it's not much of a stretch to decide which ones you want to bid on.

Now targeting is virtually the same as Google. As you can see in figure 24.4 above the 3 different targeting options you can use. As we're not a national business here and you're a local business, it's important you choose "Let me choose specific locations" and copy and paste your business address and zip code in there.

Once you've done this and as you can see in figure 24.5, you have to click on the grey dot on your screen and then click the button "Target". Now you can edit how far the radius you want to target which is very simple from there. It's a little more complicated than on Google but once you've done it, you can at the bottom of the screen make sure you ONLY tick "People in your targeted locations" otherwise everyone searching for your keywords regardless of whether they're in the radius of your practice will be able to see your ad which obviously you don't want.

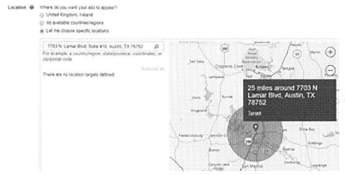

Figure 24.5 showing how to target a specific radius around your practice location/s.

World Leading Practices for Choosing Your Keywords on Bing

You will now be at keywords. Keywords are exactly the same as Google especially in terms of Exact match, phrase match, broad match modifier, broad match etc. As you can see below in figure 24.6 Bing gives you the option to create multiple ad groups at the same time which is really fantastic and saves you doing all the work after. This will save you a considerable amount of time playing around with Ad groups later   and allows you to finish setting up your campaigns much quicker. You can even get suggestions from Google on the right hand side of figure 24.6 as you can with Google but I'd recommend staying away from that.

Remember Bing and Google make 85%+ of their revenue from their advertising platform so they're going to recommend broad match keywords as they cost you much more. So ignore them and go with what I've recommended to you here. Stick with exact match & phrase match keywords.

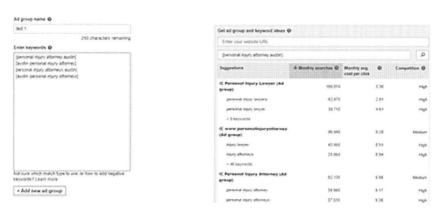

Figure 24.6 showing how to set up your keywords and ad groups in Bing.

Now the main focus of this final portion of the chapter doesn't need to be on creating ads as you can see in figure 24.7 because it's exactly the same as Google. Instead let's focus briefly on ad extensions instead because you're going to want to focus on these only:

1. Sitelink extensions.

2. Callout extensions.

3. Structure snippets extensions.

4. Location extensions.

5. Call Extensions.

6. Review extension.

Figure 24.7 shows you how simple it is to create an ad with Bing.

Now some of you may question the reason I've left out app extensions and price extensions. The reason for leaving app extensions out is a simple one: most of you are local business owners which means most of you don't have an app. Although I will say creating an app can be a fantastic way to stay top of mind of all your customers. Anyway, price extension needs more explanation. Some people will disagree with me on this because they think sharing their prices is a good idea and helps people make good decisions to work with you.

Well remember how humans make decisions? Humans make decisions 95% of the time unconsciously which means 95% of people's decisions are very quick. They aren't rational and well thought out. This is the reason your ad copy has to be on point because it's one thing to know you're acquiring quality patients and clients from Google Adwords and then your website BUT what you don't know is how many you're losing from your terrible copy.

Therefore price doesn't help a person make a decision. *The only thing price does is give the person a justification to not work with you* as most of you aren't the cheapest people to work with and why should you be? Most of you have spent at least 5 years in education and spent at least 10-30 years out of that getting better at your craft every single day. There shouldn't be any reason you charge cheaply. You're charging based on value not on how cheap you can offer it. As a result when people see your price extension they've got the information they need to then tell all their friends about how expensive you are which isn't good.

So… it's generally a very poor idea to put your prices on a price extension or on your website as a whole. On top of which most of you won't be able to give an immediate price because you haven't diagnosed what the patient or client needs most yet. Bottom line? Stick to the 6 original ad extensions and ignore app extensions and price extensions.

How to Create High Quality Copy Which Converts OVER & OVER Again on Bing

Remember our good friend copy? Well I'm going to give you another important ad copy strategy you can implement into your Bing campaigns as well as your Google campaigns.

Now you have the exact same amount of characters in your headline, description & display URL as you do with Google so there's no extra advantage on this front you get from Bing you don't get with Google.

Therefore understand the most read part of your entire ad is your headline. As you can see below in figure 24.8 the biggest part of your entire ad is your headline and as a result if people don't like your headline then don't expect them to read your description or click through to your landing page. Even if you write the greatest description in the world but have a bad headline it won't matter because people will lose attention the minute they dislike your headline.

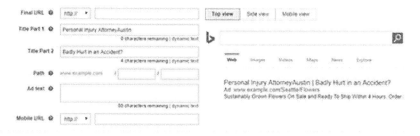

Figure 24.8 shows you how to set up a Good Headline in your search engine ads.

As a result one of the easiest ways to grab attention is through curiosity but not curiosity on it's own. Curiosity on it's own doesn't give a person a real incentive to click on your ad. People will click your ad based on curiosity if they have the time to click. They won't make the time to click. However one of the greatest incentives you can give is one of self interest and curiosity therefore the 2 combined can work wonders.

In case you're wondering the combination of both these 2 principles was created by the great John Caples in his fantastic book "Tested Advertising Methods" which I highly recommend you read. Your entire ad wants to be framed around self interest and curiosity because you're very limited on characters as it is and you need enough to get the click. Once you have the click you can go into your landing page which will complete the conversion process for you for your receptionist to then book the appointment.

So let's talk structure. Remember prospects want to feel like you understand them because once you understand a person it means you can provide a great solution. If you don't understand a person's pain or at least communicate you understand then how are you supposed to provide a quality solution? The answer is you can't provide a quality solution if you don't know what the person's pain is in the first place.

Therefore it's critical in your headline to acknowledge right away the person's pain because then you have the highest chance in getting the person to stop and read what else you have to say. Remember though headline 1 is always going to be the keyword inserted into your headline because you can't mess up your relevance. Headline 2 is where you're going to acknowledge their pain and an example could be:

1. Struggling with X?

2. Difficulty with X?

The point is I'm immediately acknowledging what the prospect's most urgent problem is they want solving right away. Remember you have 30 characters so you're going to have to play around with variations to ensure you don't go over the limit. However, one of the reasons your CTR can go low doing this even though you're acknowledging what your prospects want solving right away is because you don't acknowledge the right problem. Instead you may mention a problem most prospects are having but it isn't the most urgent one.

For example a person may have an open wound on their arm and alongside that may have a problem with their knee. But which is the most urgent? Clearly the open wound on the arm is and when you acknowledge this, a person has much more incentive to respond because it's a problem they want solving right this minute.

You're now onto the description part of the ad which is where you're going to heavily hit on:

1. Self Interest.

2. Curiosity.

We're adding in curiosity because it gives a person a higher reason to click than just self interest alone. Of course you're providing a unique solution other competitors can't provide but adding curiosity gives you a higher chance more people will click your ad and see your offer. A great example pattern you can use is:

How much better would your life be if we fixed X for you without you doing X?

OR

How much better would you feel if we quickly did X for you? Call Now for More!

What we're doing here is allowing the prospect to dream. We're allowing the prospect to go deep into their mind and ponder on their answer to this question as it's an interesting question which involves the specific outcome the prospect wants.

As we've already mentioned the problem they want solving in the headline we can now offer the solution embedded with curiosity to increase your CTR. Also notice how I'm asking a calibrated/open ended "How" question. The reason behind this is because there's significantly more answers a person can answer to this question than they can to a YES/NO question. A YES/NO question has one answer and when a question has one answer it doesn't arouse any curiosity. What arouses curiosity is when the answer could be multiple different things. *Plus we're using a question because whenever you ask someone a question their mind has to come up with an answer.* When you say a statement a person doesn't have to respond back to you and the goal of direct response marketing is to get people to respond.

How Do I Best Optimize My Bidding?

Now we're on the home straight of finishing your Bing ad campaigns. You'll be bidding on your entire campaign as you can see in figure 24.9. Just remember to make sure your bidding is "Accelerated" especially when testing to ensure you get data and results in as fast as possible. We don't want to be waiting longer than we should be to find out the result of a test. However we're now at the point of the optimal bid strategy because this is where some "experts" disagree with me. I would strongly recommend you go with "Manual Bidding" only because it keeps you in much greater control of your budget to ensure you don't blow your entire budget in 30 days. Some people recommend "Maximize Clicks" which is very similar to Facebook Advertising but stick with manual bidding. You'll benefit far more personally and so will your bank account.

Figure 24.9 showing you how to set your bid.

Now it's even more important you pay attention to what I'm about to show you. You can bid normally on each of your ad groups as you can see in figure 24.10 which is fine. What's important now is advanced targeting and advanced bidding similar to Adwords.

With advanced targeting as you can see in figure 24.11 you can see how you can increase or decrease your bids based on the area you want to target. For example you may already know a big portion of your business comes from specific neighbourhoods of the city and if that's the case you might want to increase your budget more on those areas. You might have other neighbourhoods which don't convert very well and as a result you might want to decrease your budget.

Figure 24.10 shows you how to bid based on each ad group.

Figure 24.11 shows you how to increase or decrease your bid based on each location you go after.

However I must mention the key difference between advanced bidding on Bing & Adwords because it's very easy to get this wrong. As you have such a diverse range of people who search on Google most of which search from their mobile phones which is the reason I suggest 70/30 in favour of mobile phones.

But with Bing, the audience is generally older so bidding via device varies in every case. Therefore I'd recommend leaving every single campaign as 50/50 on your bidding, letting a week or two of results come in and then make the decision to either increase, decrease or keep the the split the same on mobile phones and desktops.

Finally as you can see from figure 24.12 the 3 options on "Other Settings" you can choose from. Now on Adwords you can get away with using Search Partners which means advertising at the same time on search engines who partner with Google.

However with Bing you DO NOT want search partners turned on and instead opt for the option: "Bing, AOL, and Yahoo search (owned and operated) only" which is the one right in the middle. Trust me you'll thank me when your campaigns get lots of traffic going this route instead of getting very little traffic using search parters. Then, you're done!

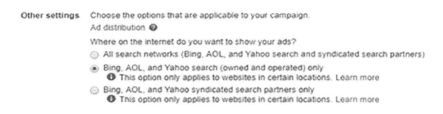

Figure 24.12 shows what networks within Bing you'd like to show your ads on.

Bing really is that simple. It's crazy to think there's a terrible assumption going around in the marketing and business arena that Bing is a completely different animal to Google. As I've just proved to you, it's evident that's the complete opposite of what's really true. Instead Bing is extremely similar to Google in how it operates, setting up your ads, bidding on keywords and managing your campaigns as a whole.

Let's now move on to the biggest video advertising platform in the world Google happens to own. If you immediately thought YouTube, you're absolutely right. Let's dive into the importance of YouTube right now.

Chapter 25

Be a Local Celebrity
with YouTube Ads

———————◆———————

Now, why YouTube ads? I'm glad you asked, well you'll want to understand YouTube is the second most viewed search engine in the world behind Google and like I mentioned with Facebook, attention is becoming more and more pronounced towards video. YouTube is all about video and quite frankly the only reason you go on YouTube is to watch videos. This is why pattern interruption is going to be everything when your ads show up before someone is about to watch a specific video of their choice.

Why Do YouTube Ads Have so Much Importance for Your Business?

Alongside this, YouTube is extremely cheap which is extremely similar to Facebook Lead Generation in the way you're able to get really cheap traffic and turn those small investments into lifetime customers. No other 2 platforms really give you the same luxury as YouTube and Facebook does. Like I mentioned above, you're wanting to enhance the omnipresence effect as much as you can so you want to be all over the platforms which are getting the most attention from prospects in your city.

The good news for you and your business is almost anything going viral in the modern age is some kind of video or some form of audio recording so why would you ever move away from 2 platforms which allow you that potential...? You don't want to give your competitors the chance of their videos going viral just because they got to the platform first. Even if you don't have the budget for YouTube ads currently and want to focus primarily on Adwords then it's a fantastic idea to start posting informative YouTube videos for your channel anyway and we'll go into the specifics of how to set your channel up most effectively.

Just posting consistent YouTube videos alone allows you to stand out above your competitors because you're giving high quality information away for free but also you can turn those videos into content for other social media channels if you'd like. Social media is out of the spectrum of this book but it's critical you start establishing a social media presence in your city. You don't have to be Kylie Jenner to start having big success using social media. The reason most fail at YouTube and other mediums is because they aren't done properly for local businesses.

What's the Best Way to Structure My YouTube Campaigns?

So Let's dive into the specifics of how to use YouTube & YouTube ads successfully for your local business. But remember this, successful people and successful businesses often times simply do the tasks and activities which the other people and businesses refuse to do. YouTube is one of those tasks. Make YouTube your friend.

First off, many of you might be wondering where the heck do you go to set up YouTube ads in the first place? Well it's very easy because YouTube is owned by Google so you only need to set up your ads in your Google Adwords account. As you can see in figure 25.1 below, you would click on "Video" to start your YouTube campaign set up.

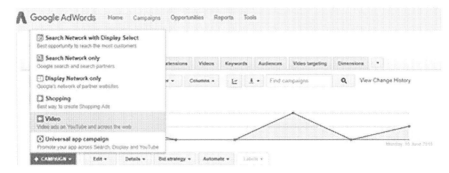

Figure 25.1 shows how to set up YouTube campaigns in the Adwords interface,

We have two specific types of YouTube ads you'll want to know about. The first are called in-stream ads which are those video ads you'll see whenever you're about to watch a video and the best example of an in-stream ad is the Tai Lopez ads you saw whenever you decided to watch a video.

The second type of YouTube ad is what's called an in-display ad which are those video ads on the right hand side of your screen whenever you're watching a video. In-display ads don't play automatically like in-screen ads do and as a local business owner it's far better to stick to in-screen ads just because you're going to generate far more attention that way. So as you can see in figure 25.2 the different option between in-stream ads and in-display ads so make sure you don't pick the wrong one.

Figure 25.2 showing how to set up in-stream and in-display ads.

Also understand in-display ads are designed to keep you on YouTube in the first place so they're not really taking you to a landing page which is the primary objective of why a local business advertises in the first place. The only exception is unless the business is spending extra money to brand themselves and build awareness which I don't suggest immediately anyway.

Now it's important you pay close attention to figure 25.3 on which networks you want to advertise on. Therefore make sure you choose "YouTube Search" & "YouTube videos" simply because you can completely mess up the amount of impressions you're getting if you use video partners in a large city. Once again I will say if you're in a much smaller city I.e. below 100,000 then video partners can work well because you're limited on traffic anyway. However if you're in a city of 100,000+ then don't use video partners.

25.3 shows you how to deselect video partners for YouTube ads.

We'll dive into how to create a highly attentive video later in this chapter but understand in-display ads are used best for branding. For example when you're wanting to increase the amount of subscribers you have on your YouTube channel. Of course you can always grow your YouTube channel slowly like most people do but if you have an extra $300 a month in order to simply grow your YouTube channel then it's worth doing providing you follow the set-up instructions which I'll lay out for you in a moment.

Like I mentioned before, successful advertising right off the bat comes down to your ability to gain attention and as you're wanting more calls and as a result more lifetime customers then you're going to want to generate as much attention as possible from your ideal prospects. This is why using in-stream ads are going to be far more helpful to you in the short and long term than in-display ads alongside the fact your money will actually be going to proper use.

So before we move into the set-up of YouTube ads for local businesses I want you to be focusing on how you can draw as much attention as possible to your business from a video as remember, you'll only have 5 seconds before the prospect has the ability to skip you. Don't forget no matter how good your intentions are, people will still skip your ad over and over again if you're not enticing enough.

How to Go About Creating a High Quality YouTube Channel

Let's talk over the set-up of your YouTube ads alongside how to create a highly attentive and good looking YouTube channel in the process. Understand if people click your ad they're either going to choose to go to your landing page or they're going to go to your YouTube channel to see what you're doing as a business. If your YouTube channel has barely any videos on it or has barely any activity then how do you think that's going to reflect on you? It's going to reflect you don't have much care to put content out for people and you're only advertising to take people's money.

When this kind of reputation starts to spread you're in for real trouble and frankly it's the same with Adwords also so make sure you've done the groundwork of setting everything up behind the scenes before heavily advertising. You'll want all of those dollars invested to be going towards as much return as possible which is why throughout this book we're focusing so heavily on minimising budget and maximising return.

Now once you've done all of that and have selected your area you want to target within a specific radius just like Adwords, we move onto targeting.

Best Practices for Leverage YouTube Targeting

Now targeting is a much different animal in comparison to Adwords because with Adwords your ads are showing up based on what a person has searched. That's simple enough right? It's one of the reasons Google & Bing are the best networks to advertise on because you find potential patients and clients who are in a much greater need for your solution. We don't have the same luxury with YouTube ads.

So as you can see in figure 25.4 the various different options you're giving for YouTube ads targeting. Now as you can see you can still bid on keywords but it's hit or miss because skill on video is a completely different conversation than ad copy on Google. That requires a completely separate book in it's own right. Therefore for local businesses using YouTube ads, it's going to be most effective if you use YouTube purely for retargeting because of how cheap it is. On top of which it's not like you're advertising to a cold audience.

Instead you're advertising to people who showed interest in your landing page as we discussed earlier but didn't convert. Just so you know this is one of the ways you really maximise ROI: by using strategic retargeting.

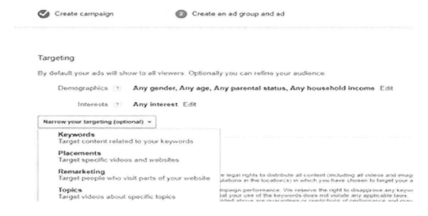

Figure 25.4 showing how to set up retargeting in YouTube.

Once you've selected retargeting as an option, pay close attention to figure 25.5. You simply have to click the drop down menu and select "Adwords remarketing lists" and the lists you've already created will show up and show you the size of the list. Select the list you want to target and then you're good to go. Now you're retargeting on both:

1. Google

2. YouTube

Figure 24.5 showing how to select the right remarketing list for YouTube.

This means no matter what happens you're going to be making sure your potential patients and clients see your ads reinforcing your unique value/unique problem over and over again until they convert.

Remember most people won't just convert on the first run. A lot of people will like what you have to offer, get distracted and won't return. Therefore retargeting will be your secret weapon in bringing considerably more high quality patients and clients into your business. On top of which we're not just retargeting. We're retargeting with the specific value you offer your competitors can't offer which is key. If you don't do this then retargeting won't nearly be as effective. You have my guarantee on that.

It's also critical we discuss how to set-up your YouTube channel in an optimal way. Your YouTube channel is just like any other social media page and if you haven't been treating it correctly then it's going to look very bad on your business when an ideal prospect visits your page and gets turned off from calling you because you didn't bother to set it up right. Trust me first impressions matter especially over the internet.

The first thing you'll want is a high quality banner image which is just like your cover photo for your Facebook page so what I recommend is using the exact same banner photo for all of your social channels so it's much easier to associate who you are. Otherwise you increase the chances of a prospect getting confused with who you are and when that happens they click away.

On top of which it's a great idea to have the same unique value or specific problem you solve your competitors can't solve on all your banners to reinforce your key message. This is so important because you want this to spread as much as possible because how people describe your business in one sentence to other people will be critical for dramatically increasing your word of mouth business.

Just like with your banner image you'll also want a high quality profile picture of you the owner and if you don't practice anymore or customers don't see you anymore as you're behind the scenes then use a quality picture of your brand logo. It's not the end of the world because your cover/banner photo will take care of humanising your business. In addition you'll want to organise all of your current YouTube videos into their own private folders so whenever someone goes to your YouTube channel it's much easier for them to access any specific video topic they want.

Often times you'll have created a video which does better than all of the others and sometimes when you type that video into the YouTube search engine it won't come up therefore it's ever more important to organise all of your videos so people can see them easier. One of your most important folders to create is "Most viewed/Most popular videos" as this will help with organisation and prospects always appreciate it when you make their life easier. It's also a great idea to use annotations on all of your normal YouTube videos and as for annotations for your ads we'll go over that in a moment as to do that is a completely different method.

If you aren't aware of what annotations are, they're those small links which show up on your screen as you watch a video which take you off YouTube and onto some other website. The reason they're effective is because even when you're just posting content for free you'll still give people the opportunity to visit your landing pages you've set up so you're not spending any money to acquire new customers and patients.

Understand annotations don't work on mobile so to counteract this you can use what we call end-screens which are annotations at the end of each video you can make which take people to specific pages you want. They do work on mobile but quite frankly test them both out and see which yields a better response for your YouTube videos. This is partly the reason why social media is so effective because when you build a reasonable audience size you're obtaining consistent customers for free without having to rely on anyone to bring you those customers.

Step by Step How to Link Your Adwords Account With Your YouTube Channel

Now, you'll want to link your Adwords account up with your YouTube channel and to do that you simply click on the right icon on your YouTube channel called:

1. "Creator studio".

2. Then click "Channel".

3. Then you'll want to click "Advanced".

4. Finally you'll want to go back into Adwords and collect your customer ID and copy and paste it into that box in YouTube we've just opened.

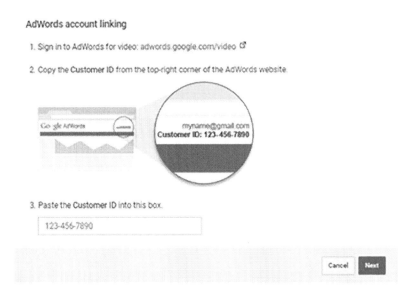

Figure 25.6: Picture of YT page for putting in Adwords Customer ID.

Understand however that you want to set Frequency capping (the amount of times someone can see your ad) to 5-7 times per week as YouTube ads can burn out extremely quickly especially for a local business if your ad is shown for any longer than that. If you're not in the office at the weekend then only shoot for 5 days as there's no point in receiving calls if you're not there to take them not to mention spending money when you're not able to capitalise on it. The last thing you want is for people to spread a negative word about constantly seeing your advertising because negative word spreads very quickly. So advertise heavily but make sure you're within the 5-7 capping ratio.

However despite all of this the billionaire dollar question is… What makes a good video ad in the first place?

This section is arguably the most important of this entire chapter. You must understand how to create highly engaging videos in the first

234

place because if you don't know how to do this then everything else including the set-up isn't going to mean much.

Understand we're gaining attention through our spoken words this time not written down copy so your tonality here is going to be so crucial in getting the attention you want.

How Can I Create Compelling YouTube Video Ads?

First off though, YouTube allows you to have call to actions through Adwords simply by going on your campaign in the campaign manager and selecting "call to action" and then doing it there. Remember this is the only text YouTube allows you to have for your in-stream ads so follow the headline formula we use for Adwords & Bing in the earlier chapters as that in itself will play it's part in attracting more attention. Therefore having a high quality attentive headline is going to be very important because if you don't have one then prospects could love your video but hate that fact they have to really look to find where to click.

The whole point of great advertising is making the process as easy as possible for prospects to find their way to the holy grail which is... giving you a call. Therefore it's important you go and study Tai Lopez's video ad I'm sure many of you saw on YouTube which is "Here in My Garage". You may be wondering why to study it?!?! The reasons it's important are because:

1. It was one of the most viral and spoken about videos of the 21st century.

2. He was inviting you to a free training and most business owners are inviting prospects to some kind of free consultation or consultation in general. Even if you're offering a paid consultation it's still the same process.

On top of this you must at the very start of your video not only say something bold but also show people something bold so they can see with their own eyes. Remember we're accommodating for auditory and visual learners here so there's no point in leaving either one of the groups out. For example a chiropractor could use a very expensive machine initially, or a dentist could show the really bad state of someone's teeth. There's many examples but you'll want to be bold and figure out what the general assumptions are of your niche and then aim to contrast that as much as you can to maintain attention.

Again Tai Lopez brought your attention to an expensive car but the assumption was rich people don't read so he contrasted the expensive car with thousands of books. You're wanting to create a similar effect to actually keep your prospect's attention because it's a massive pattern interrupt. When you do the exact opposite of people's expectations they can't help but listen to what you have to say.

Alongside this you're going to want to say multiple phrases of the same point to reduce anxiety of why someone should give you a call i.e. It's free, it's guaranteed, you don't lose anything etc to create the effect they have more to lose by not clicking to your landing page than they do of clicking it. You also must make sure you stress the call to action in your video which should be roughly 2-4 minutes long. If you can get your message across in 60 seconds that's fine also. Just don't forget the entire frame of the video is you're inviting the person back to come in for an appointment. You're not forcing them back but instead using the fact they already visited your page from Google as leverage to invite them back for an appointment. It's never a cold sell.

It's always a welcoming authoritative hand you're holding out for the person to grab onto.

Chapter 26

Concluding Each
War on Your Terms

———◆———

D am we're finally at the end. Wow that was one crazy ride we just went through and it's only going to get better for your business when you apply what we've spoken about in this book.

The Importance of Clickfraud Technology

As I've said at the beginning of this book about the importance of clickfraud technology. Seriously the amount of clickfraud going on within search engines including Bing is absolutely monstrous. What makes it worse is most business owners have no idea it's going on let alone the amount of agencies who don't serve their clients properly by dealing with it. That's like a cosmetic surgeon seeing there's something important which needs to be shaped on a person's face but doesn't do anything about it. It's not the best situation.

Fortunately for you though you know exactly how to deal with clickfraud and most importantly you're aware it's happening. A considerable amount of agencies seem to think Google is just this great company and they'd never do anything like this to anyone. I'd then ask well how do you explain Google getting fined 90+ million dollars a few years ago for clickfraud...? This usually quiets them down.

The main thing is you know the truth because once you know the truth you can start acting upon it especially business owners such as personal injury attorneys who have to spend outrageous amounts of money just for one click. For example an personal injury attorney in Denver could end up spending $250 just for one click. So how would you feel if 60-70% of your clicks weren't even real people? At this point every single attorney I've spoken to after mentioning this one point immediately wanted clickfraud right away. What sane business owner wouldn't?

How Undeniably Important Ad Copy is to Success with Google Adwords

Now it's important we also conclude with ad copy because once again this is an area most marketing agencies don't do properly. What makes it worse is the businesses which thrive on Google are the ones who have the biggest budgets, *not the ones who have the best marketing.*

One of the main purposes of this book was to ensure quality businesses didn't have to be stomped out of town on Google because they'd failed to hire a high quality marketing strategist. This brings me to another point. Your best results will almost always come from hiring one specific marketing strategist over hiring a medium sized to large agency. If you're 100% sure the person over the phone you're speaking with is the a world leading authority on Google Adwords then you'll be fine. The issue arises when you speak to someone on the sales team who's great at sales but isn't managing your campaigns. Honestly this happens 8 times out of 10 and business owners get mislead into contracts which they then can't get out of. Don't be that business owner.

Back to copy. It's critical you either study immensely what I've spoken about in this book and write copy yourself or you hire someone externally to do it. Either way if you hire someone externally to write your Adwords copy then make sure you question them fairly heavily on how they plan to write your copy because copy and clickfraud technology are going to be 2 of your biggest secret weapons in your Adwords success. Seriously they're that important so make sure you don't ever overlook the importance of these at any moment of your campaign.

On top of which copy itself should be constantly studied as much as you can every single day you run your business. Remember we're talking about Google Adwords now but in the next 20 years Google may not even exist, but copy will. Advertising copy is always going to be the same no matter what happens in the market and the only difference is going to be the medium with which the advertising is expressed through. That's the only thing which will change.

People's brains and how they're wired don't appear to be changing anytime soon and neither does advertising as a whole. As a result if there's one skill you must have above everything in marketing it's your ability to write advertising copy. Trust me this one skill alone will save you so much money and heartbreak from hiring different copywriters to work for you.

On top of which the best copywriters in the world will usually charge you a 5 figure investment and will also want at least 20% of the profits too. Plus most top copywriters likely won't write your Adwords copy because it's too minimal of a job so at this point you'd then have 3 options to consider. You could either :

1. Write the copy yourself.

2. Get very very fortunate with a marketing strategist who's just as incredible at copy as they are at Adwords.

3. You hire me depending on whether I'm already working with a competitor of yours in your city.

Not bad options right? Well make sure you pick one and it's the write one because bad advertising copy will forever drain your advertising budget regardless of how much money you spend on Google Adwords. High quality copy will always win. *You just have to make sure you find the most urgent problem your potential patients want solving.* Once you have this you're on the right path to winning.

The Enormous Potential of Adwords to Grow Your Business Regardless of No Previous Success

Finally let's conclude with the importance of Google Adwords and SEO as the two best long term marketing methods in growing your business. Now I'm not here to talk to you about SEO but simply to point to the importance of it towards scaling out your business.

Now as we've already made clear the importance of Google Adwords in growing your business simply because it's direct response marketing. A considerable amount of people who search for the specific terms you're bidding on are in need of an urgent solution and as a result want the solution right now. These make the highest quality patients and clients in the long term as they tend to be more loyal because you've helped them at a time of severe need.

Now this doesn't mean Facebook lead generation isn't important for acquiring quality patients and clients because it is. What it means is most of the time your highest quality patients will come from Google Adwords and generally you'll acquire a much higher quantity.

Now this brings us to the importance of SEO in conjunction with Google Adwords. Remember we're going after specific keywords with both methods which means when you're consistently ranking in position 1 for paid and organic search it becomes very difficult to compete against you because you occupy the most important positions for the search engine.

As I said before, bad copy leaves you vulnerable to losing your position and as a result using the copy techniques here will leave you in a very tough position to be beaten. Seriously these 2 methods alone done properly will make you millions of dollars over the long term. Not every business owner believes this when they first hear it but that doesn't take any truth away from it.

On top of which SEO is completely free which means long term it's one of the highest ROI methods you can use to grow your business. So you may think well why not skip paying for Adwords and go with SEO? Well Adwords is much FASTER in generating quality patients compared to SEO. What I will say though is it takes a long time to rank position 1 in the searches and in the maps for SEO especially if you're going after a very competitive city I.e New York, Chicago, Los Angeles etc.

So be prepared with SEO to invest a considerable amount of money upfront for the first 90-120 days with very little results to show for it. Any honest SEO strategist will explain this to you so don't worry.

So now we're at the end. It's been a super crazy journey taking you through this book and for many of you this is just the beginning of you using Adwords highly successfully. Why aim for a 500% ROI when you can acquire at least 1000% using the key methods within this book…? The methods and strategies are now laid out in this book specifically for you. All you have to do is apply them.

Hope you've enjoyed and until next time.

Callum Davies
Orlando, Florida, November 2018

Acknowledgements

---◆---

This is my second book and first ever on Google Adwords so I want to really make a point of thanking those people and mentors who have helped and encouraged me to relentlessly improve every single day. I also want to make it clear how in debt I am to the few Google Adwords geniuses who I can safely say make me a better marketer each day. This book would not be possible without them.

My biggest thanks go out to my best friend and mentor Imran Tariq. My current & future success alongside the writing of this book are all owed to him for making me an entrepreneur. I would not be in the position if it wasn't for him. I owe him the world & 100 times more for the wisdom, guidance and knowledge he has bestowed upon me and continued effort & support he continues to offer.

I'd like to thank Kyle Sulerud from Ad Leg for being one of the only Adwords marketers for local businesses who was able to provide world class information. Kyle is truly the best at what he does and I cannot thank him enough for his help & guidance to me when I was still trying to connect all the dots together.

Another person I'd like to thank who I've quoted already in this book is Brad Geddes. Brad is arguably the best search engine marketer on the planet and I offer great thanks towards him for his knowledge & wisdom in making me a better Adwords marketer every single day.

Massive thanks goes to my family and especially grandparents for their constant love & appreciation. Alongside them, a special mention goes out to my other best friend Finn. Despite seeing the evolution and completely change in me from a total nobody into an entrepreneur, I appreciate your never ending loyalty and friendship. The world wouldn't be the same without you.

40059368R00151

Made in the USA
Middletown, DE
22 March 2019